DEEP LEARNING WITH PYTHON

The Ultimate Beginners Guide for Deep Learning with Python

Table of Contents

Introduction

There has been a lot of progress made in the world of Artificial Intelligence and Machine Learning. Machine learning products such as highly sophisticated translation engines, increasingly accurate self-driving cars, intelligent conversational robots, etc. have drawn the attention of technology lovers and the general public at large to this promising field of Computer Science. Most of these products are being developed using techniques derived from a subfield of machine learning called Deep Learning. Deep learning agents have won the best humans at complex games such as chess, Go, and the popular strategy game StarCraft and are showing no signs of stopping.

If you are reading this book, there is a high probability that you are aware of a lot of these advances, and you have decided to take a step further. You actually want to understand what makes these systems work. You are probably not satisfied with simply cheering on the sidelines but want to be at the forefront of the action. If this is you, then you are with the right book.

While there has been a lot of mind-blowing progress made in the world of Deep Learning, there has also been a lot of doubt. We are beginning to understand that Deep Learning is not a silver bullet that solves every problem imaginable. We are beginning to feel out the edges of the board of problems that the current state of machine learning can be profitably applied to. This might seem like bad news but it's probably one of the best things to happen to the budding field. Instead of focusing on the hype, researchers are incentivized to double down on the range of problems that can actually be solved by deep learning, and this range of problems is ever increasing due to the publishing of quality research papers by researchers, papers that are constantly increasing in number and being backed by highly driven institutions and companies.

So while we know that deep learning probably does not solve all our problems, we've also realized that there is a huge amount of potential waiting to be explored using just the current state of the art. This state of the art of course is steadily improving.

As can be seen, it is an amazing time to be part of the machine learning community. There are lots of new solutions to be found, and lots of existing solutions to be fixed! There are also a lot of tools created by the community to ease contribution, so that if one stays committed, the person ends up building useful deep learning systems in a reasonable amount of time.

How is this book aimed at helping you? While there are lots of tools that help you build deep learning systems and there are still a lot more to come, the basics of deep learning remain fundamentally the same. As with any complex field/subject, it is always vital you understand the fundamentals first so as to be able to understand the more advanced aspects on a much deeper level. With a deep understanding of the fundamentals, one only has to pay attention to the details that make one system different from the other. In writing this book, we aim at making the reader familiar with the fundamentals of deep learning without going deeply into the Mathematics involved. To carry out this task, we will start with the definition of some important terms:

1. **Machine Learning**: Machine learning is a field under artificial intelligence that studies the approaches that are efficient at providing systems the ability to automatically learn and improve from experience without being explicitly programmed.

2. **Neural Networks**: A neural network or Artificial Neural Network (artificial neural network) is a computing system inspired by the biological neural networks that constitute animal brains. It is a network or circuit of neurons composed of artificial neurons or nodes. These nodes are used for processing information, then passing it to another 'layer' of neurons for further processing.

3. **Deep Learning**: This is simply a system of neural networks consisting of many 'layers' of neurons which processed data can be passed to for further processing.

In this book, the aim is to give the reader a grasp of the fundamentals of Machine Learning as a whole, and then diving deep into Deep Learning. Since this is a deep learning book, we will not be writing a lot of code until we get to the Deep Learning aspect of the book. If you want to skip straight ahead to the Deep Learning chapters, you always can. Though it is strongly advised that you scan through these initial chapters to have a rounded understanding of the field that Deep Learning stems from. Now that we have a definition of the above terms which will be widely used in this book, let's take a deeper dive into the first item on the list: Machine Learning.

Chapter 1

Setting Up Your
Deep Learning Environment

The first step in your deep learning journey is to actually set up your environment and that means having to install Python first, followed by the packages you are going to need. I'm going to make things a bit easier for you by using a Python package called Anaconda. Not only does this contain Python, but it also contains a text editor.

These instructions will work for Windows, Linux and Mac OS X – I'm using OS X but you can easily follow along on your platform. Let's begin.

Step One – Download Anaconda

Anaconda is free and open-source and is one of the easiest Python packages to use for deep learning.

1. Open www.continuum.io/ - this is where you download Anaconda from
2. Click the menu and click Anaconda
3. Next, click Download and the download page opens
4. Choose the download for your operating system and then choose the latest version of Python

5. Click on Graphical Installer and Anaconda will be downloaded on your system.

Step Two – Install Anaconda

For this step to work, you need to have administrative privileges on your computer. Make sure you have before you start.

1. Find the Anaconda file you downloaded and double-click it
2. The Installation Wizard will open; follow the instructions and Anaconda will be installed.

It shouldn't take any more than 10 minutes at the most and shouldn't use more than just over 1 GB of hard drive space.

Step Three – Start Anaconda and Update it

The next step is to confirm your installation and that Anaconda is up to date. Included in Anaconda is Anaconda Navigator, a series of graphical tools. This can be started quite simply from your app launcher. These tools will be used later; for now, start conda, the command line environment within Anaconda. It is fast and it is incredibly simple to use; error messages don't have anywhere to hide, and you can easily check that your environment has been installed and is working as it should.

1. Open a command line window on your computer and type in the following to check that conda is properly installed:

   conda -V

   You should see an output similar to this:

   conda 4.2.9

2. Next, confirm that you have Python properly installed by typing:

python -V

And you should see something like:

Python 3.5.2 :: Anaconda 4.2.0 (x86_64)

3. To check that the conda environment is current, type in:

conda update conda

conda update anaconda

Step Four: Confirm SciPy Environment

Now you need to confirm that you have an up to date SciPy environment. The script below will tell you the version number of the libraries you are going to need for your deep learning environment, in specific, NumPy, SciPy, Scikit-learn, Statsmodels, Pandas, and Matplotlib. Input this script by opening your text editor, and typing or copy/pasting the script in:

```
# scipy
import scipy
print('scipy: %s' % scipy.__version__)
# numpy
import numpy
print('numpy: %s' % numpy.__version__)
# matplotlib
import matplotlib
print('matplotlib: %s' % matplotlib.__version__)
# pandas
import pandas
```

```
print('pandas: %s' % pandas.__version__)
# statsmodels
import statsmodels
print('statsmodels: %s' % statsmodels.__version__)
# scikit-learn
import sklearn
print('sklearn: %s' % sklearn.__version__)
```
Save the file and call it versions.py.

Next, go to your command line and change the directory to where you saved your script. Then type in:

```
python versions.py
```
You should see something like:
scipy: 0.18.1
numpy: 1.11.1
matplotlib: 1.5.3
pandas: 0.18.1
statsmodels: 0.6.1
sklearn: 0.17.1

Step Five: Update scikit-learn
Here, we will update the main machine learning library, scikit-learn.

1. There is every chance that, by the time you download scikit-learn, it will already be out of date. To update it, use the conda command, typing the following in at the command prompt:

conda update scikit-learn

An alternative way is to update it to a specific version by typing something like:

conda install -c anaconda scikit-learn=0.18.1

Run versions.py again to make sure the installation worked and scikit-learn has been updated:

python versions.py

And you should see an updated list of libraries.

These commands can be used to update any of your libraries as and when you need to.

Step Six: Install Your Deep Learning Libraries

Lastly, we need to install some libraries, in specific Keras, TensorFlow, and Theano. These are all deep learning libraries – the recommendation is that you use Keras and then choose either Theano OR TensorFlow; Keras does not require both of these and some Windows users may find that TensorFlow is hard to install.

Install Theano like this:

conda install theano

For systems other than Windows, you can install TensorFlow like this:

conda -c conda -forge tensorflow

And install Keras like this:

pip install keras

As you did for your SciPy environment, check that all your deep learning libraries are installed and are working. Add this script to your text editor:

```
# theano
import theano
print('theano: %s' % theano.__version__)
# tensorflow
import tensorflow
print('tensorflow: %s' % tensorflow.__version__)
# keras
import keras
print('keras: %s' % keras.__version__)
```

Save it as deep_versions.py and, to run it, type the following at the command prompt:

```
python deep_versions.py
```

and you should see something like this:

```
theano: 0.8.2.dev-901275534cbfe3fbbe290ce85d1abf8bb9a5b203
tensorflow: 0.12.1
Using TensorFlow backend.
keras: 1.2.1
```

Your deep learning environment has been successfully set up.

Chapter 2

Machine Learning

As defined above, machine learning is the field that studies ways of making systems capable of learning on their own when given data. Machine Learning is divided mainly into two classes: Supervised Learning and Unsupervised Learning. We'll explain the differences between these two classes so as to build up an understanding of the foundations of our subject matter: Deep Learning. We will also be discussing a third class – Reinforcement Learning.

Supervised Learning

When the processes involved in producing output for a set of input values follows a pattern derived from the input-output mappings of prior data, the machine is said to be carrying out Supervised Learning. In supervised learning, the machine is given the 'correct' answers to problems, and when a pattern is derived (over thousands, maybe millions of data), that pattern is then applied to future input data of the same class to predict the output. The set of algorithms that perform this supervised learning are called predictive algorithms, because the machine predicts output using an already derived pattern. While this might seem quite simplistic, the application of these predictive algorithms can prove surprisingly useful. These algorithms are used in the field of healthcare for instance, to determine whether a tumor is either malignant or benign with an accuracy that beats that gotten from the close inspection of human specialists. They can also be used for other day-to-day things like the prediction of housing costs and the prediction of movements in a stock market. There are also cases where doctors predict the actual date of pregnancy using the hormonal data of the mother.

There are two main groups of supervised learning algorithms which are Classification algorithms and Regression algorithms. When Classification algorithms are applied to a dataset, they try to sort the data into categories (or classes!). Classification algorithms are the most frequently used algorithms in the field of data science and machine learning. A few examples of use cases for classification algorithms include spam detection, sentiment analysis, churn prediction and of course dog breed detection.

When Regression algorithms on the other hand are applied to datasets, they are aimed at predicting a numeric value using previously observed data. Regression algorithms have been used for problems such as Height-Weight prediction, stock price, lab results, prediction, the already mentioned house price prediction and many other interesting problems. Here we'll introduce a few actual examples of classification algorithms using python to get your hands dirty. We'll be using the popular python machine learning library sklearn. We've chosen this because of its ease of use which is very useful while just starting out in machine learning. While we will use sklearn, we highly encourage checking out other machine learning frameworks when you feel comfortable. Some of the popular frameworks are: Keras, Tensorflow, PyTorch, Caffe. Do not just read these examples. Try them out on your computer to have a less abstract feel of the powerful framework.

Some examples of classification algorithms are: Naive Bayes Classifier, Decision Trees, Random Forest, Nearest Neighbor, Support Vector Machines.

Naive Bayes Classifier

The Naïve Bayes classifier is one of our probabilistic models, used specifically for the classification tasks. It is based on Bayes Theorem, which is:

$$P(A\backslash B) = \frac{P(B\backslash A)P(A)}{P(B)}$$

That theorem can be used for finding the probability that A will happen, if B has occurred. A indicates the hypothesis while B indicates the evidence and we make the assumption that we have independent features. What that means is that, if one specific feature is present, it does not have any effect on the other and that is why it is called Naïve.

Let's understand this better using an example, the golf problem. The dataset contains data under these headings:

- Outlook – indicates the weather being rainy, sunny or overcast
- Temperature – either hot, cool or mild
- Humidity – either high or normal
- Windy – either true or false
- Play Golf – either yes or no

Given what the current conditions are, i.e. the features, we can classify if a game of golf is played or not. The dataset columns are the features while the rows are the entries and looking at row 1, we can see that, with a rainy outlook, no wind, hot temperature and high humidity, it isn't suitable for golf. Two assumptions can be made – one, that the features are independent, and second is that every feature affects the outcome equally. By that, whether it is windy or not does not have any more importance in the final decision than any other feature.

Using the golf example, we could rewrite Bayes theorem like this:

$$P(y\backslash X) = \frac{P(X\backslash y)P(y)}{P(X)}$$

We have a variable, y, which is the class variable for playing golf; this variable will represent the suitability or otherwise of playing, given what the conditions are. X is another variable representing the features or parameters.

We can give X as:

$$X = (x_1, x_2, x_3, \ldots, x_n)$$

In this formula, x_1, x_2, x_3,..., x_n are representing the features which means they can be mapped to the features listed above – outlook, humidity, etc. If we substitute for X and use the chain rule to expand, we would get this:

$$P(y \backslash x_1, ..., x_n) = \frac{P(x1 \backslash y\ P(x2 \backslash y)...P9xn \backslash y\ P(y)}{P\ (x1)P\ (x2)...P\ (xn)}$$

Now, by looking at the dataset, you would get the values for each of the features and substitute them into the above equation. For every entry, there will be no change to the denominator – it stays static. As such, we can remove the denominator and introduce a proportionality:

$$P(y \backslash x_1, ..., x_n)\ \alpha\ P(y)\ \prod_{i=1}^{n}\ P(x_i \backslash y)$$

In this, y, the class variable, has just two outcomes, either yes or no. You may come across cases where you have a multivariate classification so we would need to find class y having the maximum probability:

$$y = \text{argmax}_y\ P(y)\ \prod_{i=1}^{n} P(x_i \backslash y)$$

With this function, given the features, we can get the class.

Different Types of Naïve Bayes Classifiers

There are three main types of Naïve Bayes classifier that you will use:

15

Multinomial Naive Bayes:

Used mostly for problems of document classification, for example, which category a document belongs in, such as news, sports, etc. The features the classifier uses are the frequency of words in the given document.

Bernoulli Naive Bayes:

Similar to the multinomial classifier, this one has Boolean variables as the features. The parameters used for predicting the class variable provide only two values – yes or no. For example, if a specific word is in the document or not.

Gaussian Naive Bayes:

If the predictors are not discrete and they take up continuous values, we make the assumption that the values are samples from a Gaussian distribution. Because the values in the dataset change, the conditional probability formula changes to:

$$P(x_i \backslash y) = \frac{1}{\sqrt{2\pi\sigma_y^2}} \exp\left(-\frac{(x1-\mu y)2}{2\sigma_y^2}\right)$$

Normally, we use the Naïve Bayes classifiers in spam filtering, sentiment analysis, and recommendation systems. They are easy to implement and very fast but they have one major disadvantage – the predictors must be independent. In many real-world cases, dependent predictors are used, and this holds the classifier performance back.

Autoencoders

From time to time in the machine learning field, there are certain instances where the feature representations of the data being considered are so large that there seems to be no memory-efficient way of handling them. A facial recognition system for instance will need to save templates of each face in its database in such a manner that it will be easy to retrieve while authenticating a user. In a case such as this, saving a color image of 128 x 128, the system will need to hold 128 x 128 x 3 values which will mean 49152 float values per face! If we were to keep a mere 100 faces, that will be way too much space used up for such a relatively simple task. There has to be a better way. Autoencoders help make this a non-issue. In this technique, neural networks are designed in such a way as to force a compressed knowledge representation of the original input. If it is a case where the input features are independent of one another, compression and subsequent decompression will be a very difficult ordeal. But if it's used in a case where there exists some correlation between the input features, these similarities can be learned and ultimately used while fitting the input through the network's bottleneck. A bottleneck is a constraint placed on the amount of information that can be passed through the neural network, ensuring a learned compression of the input data.

Other Popular Supervised Learning Algorithms

These are some other algorithms that you will come across in your deep learning journey:

Linear Regression

Linear regression tends to be one of the very first machine learning models that you will come across on your deep learning journey. It is one of the simplest models, but it is the one that you need to get to grips with as it will lay the foundation for some of the other deep learning algorithms. There are two types of linear regression – simple and multiple.

Simple linear regression uses a straight line to establish the link between a pair of variables. The line that simple regression draws is the nearest to the data and it finds that by finding the intercept and the slope that do two things – define that line and keep regression errors to a minimum.

When there are at least two variables that show a linear relationship with one dependent variable, it becomes multiple regression. Analysts tend to base this type of regression on an assumption that the dependent variable and the independent variables are linked by a linear relationship, along with an assumption that the independent variables show no major correlations.

With simple regression, there is one x and one y variable; with multiple regression, there is one y and at least two x variables.

Linear regression is one of the most powerful of all machine learning techniques and it tends to be mostly used for understanding factors that have an influence on probability. For example, it is used for sales forecasting for the months ahead, by analyzing the data from previous sales. It is also used to gain some information on customer behavior, such as the purchase of certain products, average spend, and so on.

Linear regression models can be represented by this equation:
$$Y = 0_0 + 0_1 x_1 + 0_2 x_2 + \ldots + 0_n x_n$$

In this equation:
- The predicted value is Y
- The bias term is 0_0
- The model parameters are $0_1, \ldots, 0_n$
- The feature values are $x_1, x_2, \ldots, x_n$

We can also represent the hypothesis in this way:
$$Y - 0^T x$$

And in this one:
- The model parameter, which includes the 0_0 bias term, is 0
- The feature vector is x, with x0 =1

SVM (Support Vector Machine)
The idea of the SVM, or Support Vector Machine, is to locate the hyperplane in N-dimensional space, where N indicates how many features there are. The hyperplane must classify the data points distinctly.

There are multiple potential hyperplanes that could be used for separating the data point classes. The objective is to find one that shows the maximum distance in between the data points in both of the classes, i.e. it has the maximum margin. By ensuring a maximum margin, we get the reinforcement that ensures more confident classification in the future.

A hyperplane is a decision boundary, used for the classification of data points. If the data points fall to one side or the other of the hyperplane, they are attributed to a different class. The hyperplane dimension is dependent on how many features there are; i.e. if there are two input features, the hyperplane will be nothing more than a line but, if there are three features, it is a 2D plane.

The support vectors are those data points nearest to the hyperplane and they have a direct influence on the orientation and position of the place. The support vectors allow us to get a maximum margin for the classifier and, if they are deleted, the hyperplane will move in position. These data points are used for building the SVM.

KNN (K-Nearest Neighbors)
One of the simplest algorithms, KNN predicts unknown data points using k nearest neighbors. The k value is the most important factor for prediction accuracy because it uses distance functions, such as Euclidean, to calculate the distance to determine what the nearest is. It is, however, computationally expensive and data must be normalized so that all data points are brought into the same range.

Logistic Regression

We use logistic regression when we expect a discrete output, such as whether an event will occur or not, i.e. whether it will snow or not. Normally, this algorithm uses a function to push the values into a specific range, with one of the most popular being the sigmoid function. This produces as 'S' curve and is used in binary classification problems, converting values to either 0 or 1 – the probability of whether the event occurs or not. An equation for simple logistic regression might look like this:

$$y = e^{\wedge}(b0 + b1*x) / (1 + e^{\wedge}(b0 + b1*x))$$

where b0 and b1 are both constants. During the training phase, the values for the constants are calculated so that there is a minimum error between the prediction and the actual value.

Decision Tree

The decision tree algorithm is used for categorizing the population of multiple sets of data based on specified independent variables. This is normally used in solving classification problems and techniques such as entropy are used for the categorization.

Random Forest

The random forest algorithm is a collection of the decision trees with each tree attempting to 'guess' at a classification – this is known as voting. The votes from each tree are considered and the most popular is chosen for the validation.

Unsupervised Learning

While supervised learning has attracted a lot of attention to deep learning due to its promise and range of applications, it has also sprung up doubts in the minds of researchers and enthusiasts alike as to the range of problems a supervised system can solve. Since a large majority of the machine learning problems solved today are done with supervised learning, this doubt has been extended to the viability of deep learning as a whole, seeing we humans do not learn in a *supervised* manner. As humans we are capable of learning concepts, patterns, gaining insights, in a say that is in no way supervised.

Unsupervised learning does not get as much attention as supervised learning for good reasons such as its difficulty of implementation, inconsistency at producing desired results, and the challenges involved in the definition of unsupervised frameworks. Despite all these setbacks, there are a growing number of unsupervised learning techniques that perform brilliantly when tuned properly to certain problems. These instances provide clues as to the direction of future research in the field of deep learning and artificial intelligence as a whole. Here we'll introduce a few of these techniques and examples of their implementation.

Clustering

In this technique of unsupervised learning, data points are organized into classes/clusters. The members of each cluster will be closely similar to each other while being collectively dissimilar to members of other clusters. Sounds familiar? While clustering seems to be similar to classification, there are large differences between both. Here are two important differences between the two sets of algorithms:

1. Classification algorithms group data points using class labels while clustering algorithms do not use any predefined class labels and just groups them on the fly.

2. Classification algorithms make use of training samples to group the data. Clustering on the other hand does not make use of training data.

Clustering techniques are highly efficient when applied correctly. They demand little work yet produce important insight from our data. Due to this characteristic of clustering techniques, they have been applied to various problems that were previously difficult to solve. Some of these include identifying suspicious fraudulent/criminal activity when applied to fintech companies, filtering spam, grouping out network traffic and interestingly, picking out fake news. All these have similar modus operandi: watch a data stream, point out anomalous activity in the data stream. Of course this is a very simplistic description of the range of complex processes involved in the solving of these important problems. As can be seen, a firm grasp of clustering techniques can aid one to contribute meaningfully to important problems peculiar to our times.

Clustering Types

These are some of the more common clustering types you will encounter:

Hierarchical Clustering

This algorithm is used to build hierarchies of clusters and it starts by using all the data assigned to a specific cluster. With hierarchical clustering, two clusters close to each other will be placed in the same cluster and the algorithm finishes when there is just a single cluster remaining.

K-means Clustering

An iterative clustering algorithm, K-means is designed to help you find the biggest value in each iteration. To start with, you choose the number of clusters you want. The data points need to be clustered into k groups; the larger the k, the smaller the groups and the more similar granularity whereas a smaller k means the groups are larger and with less granularity.

The algorithm outputs a group of labels. A data point is assigned to one k group; defining each group means creating a centroid for each one. These centroids are the core of the cluster, capturing the closest points to them and adding them into the cluster.

K-means also defines two more subgroups:
- Agglomerative
- Dendrogram

Agglomerative clustering

Agglomerative clustering begins with a specified and fixed number of clusters; all data is allocated into the fixed number. There is no need to input the number of K clusters as the process begins by forming the data into one cluster. It does use distance measures, it reduces the clusters by one each iteration, ending in one cluster that has all the objects.

Dendrogram

In this algorithm, every level is representative of a potential cluster. The height of the algorithm displays the similarity level between two of the join clusters. The nearer the bottom, the more similar the clusters; this is what the dendrogram finds from the group.

K- Nearest neighbors

Otherwise known as KNN, this algorithm is one of the simplest and is a classification algorithm. Unlike other algorithms, this one doesn't produce a model. Instead, it stores the available cases, using a similarity measure to classify all new instances. It works best when the examples have some distance between them as it learns very slowly on large training sets; it also has a nontrivial distance calculation.

Association

Association is another technique of unsupervised learning in which rules are created which try to establish associations amongst data points in large databases. The aim of this technique is to discover the underlying relationships between the objects in large databases. A popular use of association rule learning is grouping buyers based on their perusing and purchasing patterns. In a store for example, cooking utensils are placed in the same aisle, cosmetics have their own place, etc. The placing of items in this manner, while also making things more organized and logical, reminds the customer of items in the same class that the customer might as well just purchase seeing they are already in the store. Association techniques discover such relationships between data points in huge databases. While it might seem to be the case, association rules do not discover the preference of an individual, rather it finds the relationships between groups of elements of each transaction. This attribute is what differentiates association from collaborative filtering. Association rules can also be used to spot out anomalies (fraud) in credit card transactions.

Supervised vs Unsupervised

Before we move onto reinforcement learning, we'll take a quick look at the differences between supervised and unsupervised learning, and how unsupervised learning is used:

Parameters	Supervised	Unsupervised
Input data	Training with labeled data labeled data	Training with unlabeled data
Computational Complexity	Much simpler	Highly complex
Accuracy	High level of accuracy	Not so accurate

Unsupervised Machine Learning Applications

Some of the applications of unsupervised learning are:

- Clustering algorithms split datasets automatically into subgroups, based on similarities

- Anomaly detection will find any data points that might be unusual and is good for detecting fraudulent transactions

- Association mining can detect sets of items that occur in your dataset together

- Latent variable models are generally used for the preprocessing stage and can be useful for decomposing datasets into several components or reducing how many features there are.

Reinforcement Learning

A lesser used, more complex version of machine learning, reinforcement learning is all about taking the right action to get the maximum reward. It is used by machines and software to find the best path in any given situation and it differs from supervised learning in one key way – with supervised learning, the answer key is in the training data, meaning the model is trained on the right answer; with reinforcement learning, there isn't an answer; the model itself decides how to perform the task and, because it doesn't have a training dataset, it learns from its own experience.

As an example, we have a reinforcement agent and we have a reward – between the two are a number of hurdles. It's up to the agent to find the best path to the reward. Let's say that we have a robot. It needs to get to a diamond, its reward, but the way ahead is fraught with danger – fire. The robot will learn the correct way by trying all the paths and then picking the one that gets it to the reward with the least amount of hurdles. Each correct step rewards the robot and each incorrect one subtracts from the reward – when it reaches the diamond, the total reward is calculated based on the number of right and wrong steps.

Reinforcement vs Supervised Learning

There are a couple of very important distinctions between reinforcement and supervised learning:

- **Reinforcement -** is about making sequential decisions. The output is dependent on the current input state and the following input will depend on the output of the previous input.

- **Supervised** – whereas the decision in supervised learning is made using the input provided at the start

- **Reinforcement** – the learning decision is a dependent decision, so labels are provided to sequences of the dependent decisions

- **Supervised** – the decisions are all independent of one another and each decision is given is own label

Reinforcement Learning Types

There are two reinforcement learning types:

Positive

Defined as when event happens because of specific behavior and the frequency and strength of that behavior is increased, i.e. a positive effect. The benefits of this are that performance is maximized and change can be sustained over a long period of time. However, too much reinforcement could result in overloaded states and this has a negative effect on the results.

Negative

Defined as a behavior being strengthened because negative conditions are avoided or halted. The benefits of this are an increase in behavior and defiance being provided to the minimum standard of performance. The downside, however, is that negative reinforcement will only provide enough of the minimum behavior to be met.

Chapter 3

───────────•─•─◆─•─◆──────────•─◆

Neural Networks

As explained in the introductory section of this book, neural networks are an essential concept to grasp in order to understand Deep Learning. Fundamentally, they are the stuff Deep Learning is made up of. Neural networks are algorithms that are modeled after the human brain. These networks are set up to recognize patterns and the patterns to be recognized are received in the form of vectors/tensors (hence, TensorFlow), which means whatever form the input exists originally—sound, images, text—it has to be converted computationally into vector form. This process of turning input to be fed into a neural network into vectors is called Vectorization.

Components of Neural Networks

Deep Learning is basically an official name for stacked neural networks, which are neural networks made up of many layers. These layers each consist of nodes. A node, (slightly similar to a neuron in the human brain which fires on the event of stimuli) is where computation takes place.

Neural networks generally consist of large numbers of artificial neurons ranging from dozens to hundreds, thousands and even millions. These neurons called units are arranged in a series of layers, each connecting the layers on either side. A subset of these layers, called 'input units' are positioned to receive different forms of input from the necessary for the solving of the problem being worked on. Output units on the other hand, observe the workings of the input units and try to map out the signals the input units derive from the data being processed. One or more layers of units exist between the input and the output units, called the hidden units. For a neural network to be fully connected means that for every layer that forms the neural network, every node in such layer is connected to every node in its neighboring layers. Connections between the input unit, hidden units and the output unit are represented by numbers called weights which can either be positive or negative values. Where the values are negative, one unit suppresses another, and where the values are positive, one unit enhances or excites another. The greater these values, the greater the influence a unit has on another. This technique is inspired by the way synapses work in the organic brain.

Nodes combine the input derived from the data with these weights, which either amplifies or dampens the input depending on its perceived significance.

How Neural Networks Learn

There are different types of neural networks which have different techniques applied to them, which turn them into effective learning systems. One of these techniques is called the feedforward neural network. In this learning technique, information goes through neural networks in only one direction: information patterns are fed into the neural network through the input units which trigger the layers in the hidden units, and when the information has been changed by being acted on by these layers, the resulting output is passed on to the output unit.

Anatomy of a Neural Network

As you may have noticed, training a neural network comprises mainly of having the following properly in place:

- Layers, which represents the different transformations the input data should go through
- The input and corresponding output meant to be fed to the model
- The optimizer, which is the technique the model should 'learn' with

Neural networks generally consist of layers which when linked together, maps out the transformation processes the input has to go through to aid the system to predict an output. A loss function is then used to compare these predictions to the actual output as represented in the dataset, thereby producing a reduction value, which is technically a measure of how well the predictions made by the system matches the correct values as determined by samples in the training dataset. The optimizer makes use of this loss function to upgrade the system's weights.

Different layers take in tensors in varying formats which are in turn made to undergo different forms of data transformation. For example, easy vector data, saved in two-dimensional tensors with shape (samples, attributes), can be transformed by layers that are densely attached, also known as layers that are fully connected (the Dense layer in Keras). Sequential data, saved in 3-dimensional tensors of silhouette (samples, timesteps, attributes), is usually processed with recurrent layers like an LSTM (Long Short-Term Memory) layer.

An analogy which provides for a deeper understanding of layers in neural networks is to view them as LEGO bricks when liked to deep learning, and this analogy made very obvious when working with such a framework as Keras. The configuration of layers in neural networks using Keras is carried out by placing collectively compatible layers with the aim of creating effective and efficient pipelines for the transformation of data. The phrase 'layer compatibility' here is used to draw your attention to the design that each layer which takes part in the transformation process is strictly designed to receive tensors of some specified shape which will also only yield output tensors with a specific shape. Let us express it in a more concrete manner using actual Keras code:

```
from keras import layers
layer = layers.Dense(32, input_shape=(784,))
# A dense Keras layer containing 32 output units
```

In this instance, we have created a layer which is designed explicitly to accept only 2D tensors which have an initial dimension of 784 (note that the second dimension (2nd axis for batch) in this instance is not specified, meaning that any value given for that axis will be accepted), as input. The output this layer produces will in turn be a tensor whose first dimension has changed to become 32.

Therefore, the only layer that can be connected to this layer has to be a layer that occurs downstream and that is designed to receive 32-dimensional vectors as input. But one fundamental advantage of using Keras is this: when implementing a model, Keras is built in such a way that it takes away the burden of worrying about compatibility, since the layers we append to our models seem to be dynamically configured to perfectly align with the shape of the layer that is incoming. Take the following lines of code for example:

```
from keras import models
from keras import layers
model = models.Sequential()
model.add(layers.Dense(32, input_shape=(784,)))
model.add(layers.Dense(32))
```

As seen above, the layer that comes second in this example did not require an input_shape argument, rather it seems to automatically infer the shape of the input as being equal to the shape of the output produced by the layer which came before it.

This occurrence is very common in instances of neural networks that consist of a linear sequence of layers, having one input mapped to one output. As we go along, you are going to be introduced to a wider range of network configurations which will include:

- Networks with two branches
- Multihead networks
- Inception cubes

The configuration of each neural layer defines a theory space. It is very helpful to say machine learning is a technique which involves searching for concise and compressed representations of input data, confined to a predefined area of possibilities, with the entire process being directed by values from the feedback sign. What you will then be hunting for is a fantastic pair of values to your weight tensors involved with those tensor operations.

Deciding what your network architecture should consist of can be considered more an art than a science; and even though there are many laid out best practices and fundamentals it is possible to depend on, just practicing and reviewing (educated trial and error) is the most dependable means by which you can turn yourself into a high performing neural-network architect. The next couple of chapters is aimed at teaching you the required technical foundation for constructing neural networks and also allow you to develop intuition regarding what works or does not work for particular problems.

Loss Functions and Optimizers

When the system structure is defined, you still need to select two things:
- Loss function (objective function): This refers to a quantity that our model will aim at minimizing during the training

session. The loss function stands as an objective measure of how well our model carries out the job at hand.

- Optimizer: The optimizer determines the approach the system will take to upgrade itself depending on the loss function. Optimizers generally apply a particular form of a technique in mathematics called the stochastic gradient descent.

A neural network which gives out a lot of output will also have a lot of loss functions (meaning one loss function per output). Nevertheless, the gradient-descent process has to be determined by a single scalar loss value; therefore, for multi loss systems, all of the losses are collapsed (by means of averaging) to a single scalar quantity.

One reason it is very important that you select the most appropriate goal function for every problem you are working on is that your system will exploit every shortcut it discovers to decrease the loss; so in a case where the objective does not fully correlate with the achievement required for the job at hand, the neural network is going to wind up cutting corners and trying all the wrong means of reducing the loss, which is certainly not what we want to happen. Take for instance a stupid yet omnipotent machine learning agent trained using the Stochastic Gradient Descent (or SGD), which has been given this naively chosen goal: to implement the most efficient tactic aimed at maximizing the average wellbeing of every human that is alive. In a bid to achieve this goal in the most efficient manner, this not so bright omnipotent machine learning agent may decide that the best way of getting this done is to eliminate every human except a small group, then concentrate fully on improving the wellbeing of the lucky group that is left after the massacre, since technically, average well-being is not defined as being negatively influenced by the number of people destroyed. This was certainly what the hapless machine learning researcher or practitioner had in mind! Try not to forget that the neural networks you create will definitely be extremely ruthless in the pursuit of reducing their loss function, so always try to choose your targets sensibly and as explicitly as possible, else you find yourself having to contend with the unintended repercussions of your omission, which is not at all a rare occurrence in the practice of machine learning.

As an illustration, you will be using binary cross-entropy to attempt to solve a classification problem that involves sorting input given into one of two classes called two-class classification, use a technique called categorical cross-entropy to solve a multi-class classification problem, use mean-squared error (MSE) to solve a regression problem, use the Connectionist Temporal Classification technique to solve a sequence learning problem etc. Try not to forget that when you are working on new study problems, that you have got to think of your own goal functions. In the next chapters to come, we will try to be specific about what functions to select when working on different common (frequently encountered) machine learning problems.

First, let's discuss a couple of the more common types of loss function:

Regression Loss Functions

Mean Square Error

Also known as the Quadratic Loss or L2 Loss, the formula is:

$$MSE = \frac{\sum_{i=1}^{n}(yi - ŷi)2}{n}$$

The name tells you that the measurement for this loss function is the average of the difference (squared) between the predicted and the actual observations. It has just one concern – average error magnitude, regardless of direction. However, because the average is squared, those predictions which are a long way from the actual values will be heavily penalized compared to those that are nearer. And, MSE also some neat properties which make calculating gradients a whole lot easier:

import numpy as np

y_hat = np.array([0.000, 0.166, 0.333])
y_true = np.array([0.000, 0.254, 0.998])

def rmse(predictions, targets):
    differences = predictions - targets
    differences_squared = differences ** 2
    mean_of_differences_squared = differences_squared.mean()
    rmse_val = np.sqrt(mean_of_differences_squared)
    return rmse_val

```
print("d is: " + str(["%.8f" % elem for elem in y_hat]))
print("p is: " + str(["%.8f" % elem for elem in y_true]))

rmse_val = rmse(y_hat, y_true)
print("rms error is: " + str(rmse_val))
```

Mean Absolute Error

Also known as the L1 loss, the mathematical formula is:

$$MAE = \frac{\sum_{i=1}^{n}|yi - \hat{y}i|}{n}$$

The measurement for the mean absolute loss is the sum (squared) of the absolute difference between the predicted and the actual observations. In the same way as MSE, this also provides a measurement of the error magnitude without considering direction but, unlike the MSE, MAE requires tools that are more complicated for computing the gradients, such as linear programming. And MAE is more powerful to the outliers because it doesn't use square:

```
import numpy as np

y_hat = np.array([0.000, 0.166, 0.333])
y_true = np.array([0.000, 0.254, 0.998])

print("d is: " + str(["%.8f" % elem for elem in y_hat]))
print("p is: " + str(["%.8f" % elem for elem in y_true]))

def mae(predictions, targets):
    differences = predictions - targets
    absolute_differences = np.absolute(differences)
```

mean_absolute_differences = absolute_differences.mean()
return mean_absolute_differences

mae_val = mae(y_hat, y_true)
print ("mae error is: " + str(mae_val))

Mean Bias Error

This isn't as commonly used in machine learning, but you still need to be aware of it. MBE is much like MSE but with one difference – no absolute values. This means that we need to be cautious because it is possible that positive and negative errors could be canceled out by one another. Although they are not so accurate, the MBE may be able to determine if a model has a negative or positive bias.

The formula is:

$$MBE = \frac{\sum_{i=1}^{n}(yi - \hat{y}i)}{n}$$

Classification Loss Functions

Hinge Loss

Also known as the multi-class SVM loss function. With this loss function, the score for the correct category should be more than the sum of the scores for all the wrong categories by a margin of at least one. The hinge loss tends to be used for maximum-margin classification problems, with the most common one being the SVM, or support vector machines. It is a convex function, although it isn't a differential, and is easy to use with convex optimizers.

The formula is:

$$SVM\ LOSS = \sum_{j \ne yi} \max* 0, \ S_j - S_{yi} + 1$$

Cross-Entropy Loss

Otherwise known as the negative log-likelihood loss function, the cross-entropy loss function is the commonest setting for any classification problem. The loss increases as the probability that is predicted starts to diverge from the label.

The formula is:

$$CrossEntropyLoss = (y_i\log(\hat{y}_i) + (1 - y_i)\log(1 - \hat{y}_i))$$

There is something of note here – when the proper label is ($y(i) = 1$), the latter part of the function will disappear; when the label is $0(y(i) = 0)$ the first part of the function disappears. What is happening here is that the log of the 'actual predicted probability' is multiplied for the ground truth class. One important thing here is that this loss function will heavily penalize predictions that are confident but are not right.

```
import numpy as nppredictions = np.array([[0.25,0.25,0.25,0.25],
                [0.01,0.01,0.01,0.96]])
targets = np.array([[0,0,0,1],
                [0,0,0,1]])def cross_entropy(predictions, targets, epsilon=1e-
10):
    predictions = np.clip(predictions, epsilon, 1. - epsilon)
    N = predictions.shape[0]
    ce_loss = -np.sum(np.sum(targets * np.log(predictions + 1e-5)))/N
    return ce_losscross_entropy_loss = cross_entropy(predictions, targets)
print ("Cross entropy loss is: " + str(cross_entropy_loss))
```

How Neural Networks Differ From Rule-Based Computing

In order to acquire a well-rounded understanding of artificial neural networks, it is important first of all to understand the approach of conventional 'serial' computers and its software takes at processing data. Serial computers are equipped with a central processor which among other things, holds an array (or list) locations (or addresses) in memory, where data and instructions are meticulously arranged. Computations are then carried out by the processor which goes on to read instructions and in general any data that instruction requires to be completely carried out, from these 'addresses' in memory. This instruction retrieved is consequently executed and the results derived from the execution are stored in pre-specified memory locations for subsequent retrieval. As can be deduced, the computational steps in a serial system (and even in the standard parallel system as well) are fundamentally sequential, logical and deterministic, and it is possible to track the current state and attributes of a given variable as operation after operation acts on it.

Artificial neural networks on the other hand, are neither sequential nor necessarily deterministic. There is no need for a complex central processor when dealing with artificial neural networks, rather there are many simple central processors which are generally designed to carry out no other task but to retrieve the weighted sum of their inputs from neighboring processors. Artificial neural networks do not work by executing well-defined instructions; they are rather designed to respond in parallel (actually or in simulation) to the pattern of inputs it is presented with. Thus, there is no need for the system to have separate memory addresses where data is to be stored. Rather, data is stored and encapsulated in what can be described as the overall activation 'state' of the network. The concept of 'Knowledge', therefore, has its representation in the network itself, which when properly aggregated, is greater than all its individual parts put together.

The Limitations of Artificial Neural Networks

There seems to be a lot of benefits and constraints to the evaluation of neural networks and to lay out the advantages and limitations of neural networks with any degree of success, we have to first of all try to thoroughly examine each type of neural network, which is beyond the scope of this book. With regard to neural networks that use backpropagation nonetheless, there are a few potential problems that beginner machine learning/deep learning engineers need to know about:

- Besides explicitly specifying the overall architecture of a system and generally trying to generalize it using a random amount, the consumer serves no other purpose than to act as an input route for the data which observes it, trains the data and then has to wait for the output. In practice though, it has been stated that when using backpropagation for machine learning, "you nearly do not understand what you are doing". The community 'IS' the last equation of this connection.

- A large proportion of the time, neural networks based on backpropagation are actually really slow to train in comparison with other kinds of neural networks and sometimes have to run through tens of thousands of epochs (or learning iterations) before getting a reasonably accurate neural network. If you are to operate on a parallel computer system then it seems that this matter doesn't pose an obstacle, but it may take some time for the BPNN to be simulated on a normal serial machine (i.e. one SPARC, Mac or PC). This is only because the CPU computers have to calculate each node's use and connect separately, which with a lot of data is difficult in very large networks. On the other side, the frequency of most devices current is that this is not usually an issue.

Advantages of Neural Networks Over the Rule-Based Algorithms

You can usually expect a system to train very beautifully based on the personality of the program and the potency of the internal data patterns. This refers to problems where the connections may be somewhat vigorous or nonlinear. Artificial neural networks provide an analytical solution to traditional techniques often confined to strict assumptions of normality, linearity, changing autonomy, etc. As an artificial neural network can capture many kinds of links, it enables the consumer to mimic events rapidly and comparatively easily that could have been quite difficult or could not explain differently.

Chapter 4

∙┈∙╍∙━━∙━●━∙━●━∙━●━∙━━∙╍∙┈∙

Introduction to RNNs and LSTMs

Two very important parts of deep learning are the RNN, or Recurrent Neural Network, and the LSTM – Long-Short Term Memory. An LSTM is a type of RNN, but both are different and, in this section, I'll explain the difference to you.

Recurrent Neural Networks

When you think, you don't do it from scratch every second of the day. Every word you read is understood based on how you understood the previous words. We don't throw everything we hear or read away and start again; we have something that a traditional neural network does not have – persistence.

This is a real shortcoming and can cause problems. For example, let's say that you want to classify the types of events occurring at every single point in a movie. We can't clearly see how traditional neural networks can use reasoning about events that occurred previously in the film to predict or classify future ones.

What is needed to address this is the recurrent neural network, a neural network that contains loops. These loops are what allow the

45

persistence of information. In short, the loop will let the information pass between network steps.

RNNs look a little mysterious but, if you stop and think about it, they are not much different to a traditional neural network. You could think of the RNN as being several copies of one network, each copy passing a message on to the next copy. If we unrolled the loop in the RNN, we would see a structure that looks much like a chain.

It is this structure that tells us the RNN is very closely related to the list and the sequence we all know so well. They are, in fact, the natural structure for a neural network to use for this kind of data.

Over the years, the recurrent neural network has been applied, with huge success, to several types of deep learning problem, including language modeling, speech recognition, captioning images, language translation, and so on. The one thing that the success of the RNN depends on is the LSTM, a special type of RNN that works better than a standard RNN for many different tasks.

Long-Term Dependencies

One of the major appeals of the recurrent neural network is that they can connect information learned earlier to present tasks. For example, video frames. Understanding previous ones help us to understand the current frame. If an RNN could do this, it would be incredibly useful, but they can't. can they?

Well, that all depends on the task and the situation. On occasion, to do a task we would only need to glance at the previous information. Let's say that we have a language model that is attempting to predict the next word in a sequence based on the previous words. If, for example, we wanted to predict the next word in the sentence, "the clouds are in the …", we don't really need any other context – it is pretty obvious the next word is "sky". In cases where there is a small gap between the information that is relevant and the place where that information is required, an RNN can learn that it needs to use previous information.

There will always be cases where more context is required. Think about this sentence – "I grew up in Spain … I speak fluent …". Reading the previous information available it is fairly obvious that the missing world will be a language. But what if you wanted to narrow the actual language down? You would need to use the context of Spain, further back in the sentence. It is possible that there could be a large gap between the relevant information and the place where that information is needed and, as that gap widens, the RNN cannot learn how to connect information dots together.

Theoretically, the RNN is perfectly able to handle these long-term dependencies. After all, humans could select parameters so the RNN could solve these problems. In practice, the RNN seems incapable of learning them. The LSTM does not suffer from this problem.

LSTM Networks

The LSTM, or Long-Short Term Memory, is a type of RNN that is perfectly able to learn these long-term dependencies. Introduced in 1997, they have since been much refined and made popular, working incredibly well in many different types of problem.

The LSTM was designed explicitly to get around the long-term dependency problem and, by default, they will remember information for a long time, not having to learn it over time.

Every RNN has a chain format, a series of modules that repeat themselves and, in a normal RNN, the structure of the module is simplicity itself, perhaps just one tanh layer. In short, they have just one layer. The LSTM also has the same structure, but the module is structured differently. Rather than just one neural layer, the LSTM has four of them, each interacting with the others in a special way.

The Core Idea

There is one important factor in an LSTM – the cell state. This is much like a store's conveyor belt, running down through the whole chain with a few linear interactions, just small ones. Information can flow along the chain without being changed.

LSTMs can add information and they can remove it from the cell state, and this done in a regulated and structured way using gates. Gates are another optional way of allowing information to go through and they are made of a single multiplication operation and a sigmoid neural layer.

The sigmoid layer will output numbers that fall between zero and one, at the same time, describing the amount of each component to go through the gate. Zero indicates that nothing goes through while one indicates that it all goes through. LSTMs will have three of these, allowing them to protect the cell state and to control it.

LSTM Variants

Not all LSTMs are standard; the differences may be minor, but they are there, just the same. One variant adds something called 'peephole connections which allow the gate layers to see the cell state. Another variant uses coupled input and forget gates. Rather than deciding separately what needs to be forgotten and what should be given new information is tedious at times so using these coupled gates, those decisions can be made at the same time. In short, we forget only when an input is being used in its place and new values are input to the state only when something older is forgotten.

Another, more dramatic, variant, is the GRU, or Gated Recurrent Unit. This places the input gates and the forget gates into one gate called an update gate. On top of that, the cell and hidden states are merged, along with a couple of other minor changes, resulting in a simple LSTM model that has fast become very popular.

There are other variants, but these are the notable ones; most are pretty much the same, it's just a case of choosing the variant that works best for the problem at hand.

LSTMs do work much better for some problems and are a huge step forward in the results that we can achieve with the RNN. Of course, the next question would be, can we go any further? A common opinion seems to be that we can, and the next step is 'attention'. The idea is that every RNN step picks specific information from a bigger set. For example, if your RNN is creating image captions, it could choose a specific section of the image to examine for each word output. The last couple of years have seen LSTMs and RNNs come on in leaps and bounds and the future is looking pretty exciting indeed.

Chapter 5

Deep Learning

This is a promising part of artificial intelligence that reproduces human brain functions in processing information and generating patterns to be used in decision-making. The field of deep learning is one under the broad field of artificial intelligence (Artificial Intelligence) machine learning that comprises of networks having the ability to learn from unstructured information without supervision. Deep learning is also called deep neural learning and deep neural networks.

Deep learning was developed in conjunction with our digital age, which has triggered the explosion of information from every section of the globe in all types. This very large data, known also by "big data", has been derived from, among others, resources such as social media, e-commerce platforms, search engines, and internet cinemas. This huge corpus of data is readily available and can also be communicated by fintech software such as cloud computing.

On the other side, this data, which is usually unsorted, is so large that human understanding and extracting relevant information could take centuries. Companies understand the great potential that can be produced by unraveling this data abundance and are largely adjusting for automatic assistance to Artificial Intelligence systems.

Deep learning learns from huge quantities of unstructured data that would usually take decades of understanding and processing by humans.

Machine learning is one of the most common Artificial Intelligence methods used to process big info, a self-adaptive algorithm that becomes progressively better with experience or using freshly added data.

If a digital payment business wished to identify in its own scheme the incidence or potential for fraud, it could use machine learning programs for this purpose.

The computing algorithm integrated into a computer model processes all trades that occur on the digital platform, finds trends in information collection, and points out any anomaly that the design detects.

Deep learning, a subset of machine learning, uses a hierarchical degree of artificial neural networks to tackle the machine learning operation. Like the human mind, the artificial neural networks are constructed along with neuron nodes linked like an internet. While traditional apps create a linear analysis of data, the hierarchical feature of deep learning systems allows computers to process data using a nonlinear strategy.

A standard strategy to identifying fraud or money laundering can trust the quantity of trade that follows, while a deep nonlinear learning method would include time, geographic place, IP address, retailer type, and any other feature that is likely to point to fraudulent action. The neural network's main layer processes a raw information input such as transaction amount and moves as an output signal to another layer. The second layer processes the data of the prior layer by including extra data such as the IP address of the user and moves on its outcome.

The following layer requires information from the second layer and contains raw data such as geographic place, making the blueprint of the machine even better.

Deep learning is strongly connected with a category of brain development ideas proposed by cognitive neuroscientists in the early 1990s (particularly neocortical growth). These developmental variants share the property that proposed different learning dynamics within the mind (e.g., a nerve growth factor tide) to encourage self-organization somewhat similar to the neural networks used in deep learning variants.

Neural networks, like the neocortex, use a set of layered filters where each layer considers data from a previous coating (or working environment), then move its output (and possibly the initial input) to additional layers.

This method produces a stack of transducers that are self-organizing, well-tuned for their operating setting. A description of

1995 said,".. the baby's brain seems to be arranging itself under the impact of waves of so-called trophic factors... separate regions of the mind become connected, with a single layer of tissue aging before another and so on until the whole brain is older.

Several methods are used to explore the plausibility from a neurobiological view of deep learning variants. On the one side, it suggests several variants of this backpropagation algorithm to increase its handling accuracy. Other researchers claim that unsupervised types of deep learning could be getting closer to the biological truth. In this respect, neurobiological proof of sampling-based processing in the cerebral cortex is connected with generative neural network models.

Although there has not yet been proven a systematic contrast between the individual brain organization and neuronal encoding in deep networks, many analogies are noted. The computations conducted by deep learning elements, for example, may well be similar to those of true neurons and neuroglial residents. Similarly, the depictions produced by deep learning models are very comparable to those measured in both the single-unit and the level of individuals in the primate visual system.

Difference Between Deep Learning And Conventional Machine Learning

Deep learning has become the ideal method for most Artificial Intelligences in recent years. Classic machine learning is overshadowed. Deep learning has proved its superior effectiveness repeatedly for a multitude of functions, including speaking, natural language, vision and play. However, while deep learning does have such high efficiency, it still has a few benefits to using classic machine education and certain situations in which something like linear regression or a decision-making tree would be much better than a large deep network.

We will compare deep learning with classical machine learning in this section and contrast them with it. This will help us to define the advantages and disadvantages of both methods.

Advantages of Deep Learning over Classical Machine Learning

Amazing performance: In many areas, such as speech processing, natural language, sight, and play, deep network accuracies are far more than classic machine learning techniques. Classical machine learning cannot even compare in many situations. The following chart demonstrates, for instance, the precision of the classification of a picture of various techniques in the ImageNet data; the blue color is used to indicate traditional machine learning and the red color is a profound CNN. Classical machine Learning in this case far surpasses deep learning.

They effectively scale with information: deep networks tend to scale with more information than traditional machine learning algorithms much better. The diagram below illustrates this simply but effectively. Often, it is only to use additional information to enhance the exactness of a deep network! This fast and simple fix does not work almost as well with classic machine learning algorithms and more complicated techniques are often necessary for improved precision.

You do not need feature engineering: Classical Machine Learning algorithms often need complicated engineering of features. Usually, the information is first analyzed in the deep dive exploration system. For simpler processing, a dimensional reduction could then be made. Finally, to transfer the finest characteristics to the Machine Learning algorithm, carefully chosen. It doesn't need to be done with a deep neural network, as information can only be directly transferred to the neural network and generally perform well right outside the boat. This eliminates completely the large and demanding process engineering phase.

Easily transferable: Deep neural learning methods may be much easier than classic Machine Learning algorithms tailored to distinct domains and use cases. First of all, transfer learning enables the use of already trained deep neural networks within similar fields/sectors, for distinct apps. For instance, already trained neural networks for the classification of images tend to be used to extract object recognition networks from the front end of the computer vision. The utility of these already trained networks as an abstraction facilitates the entire model training and generally helps to accomplish greater efficiency in less time. Furthermore, the same fundamental concepts and deep learning methods used in various fields can often be transferred. For instance, once you know the foundational theory of deep learning for speech recognition, it isn't too complicated to learn how exactly to make use of deep neural networks to the problem of NLP as basic learning is quite identical. This isn't the case with classical Machine Learning since the construction of high-performance Machine Learning models requires application-specific and domain-specific Machine Learning methods and characteristic engineering. Classical Machine Learning knowledge base is quite distinct for various fields and applications, often requiring comprehensive specialist research across each region.

Advantages of Conventional Machine Learning Over Deep Learning

Performs better when given small data: Deep networks involve enormous data sets to accomplish high efficiency. 1.2 million pictures formed the previously described networks that have been pre-trained. These big datasets tend to not be easily accessible for many apps and are costly and time exhaustive to acquire. Classical Machine Learning algorithms often exceed deep networks for larger datasets.

Computationally and financially cheap: Most deep neural networks can only be trained by means of high-end GPUs with large information for a fair period of time. These GPUs tend to be very costly but would not be practically viable without training deep neural networks to perform. A quick SSD storage, CPU and quick and wide RAM are also needed to efficiently use such high-end GPUs. With just a good CPU, classical Machine Learning algorithms have been properly trained without the finest hardware.

Since they are not computer-priced enough, in a shorter time span you can generally iterate and test many distinct methods.

More accessible: These algorithms are very simple to interpret and comprehend because of their direct function engineering in classical Machine Learning. Additionally, it is easier to adjust hyperparameters and modify the model models, since the information and the algorithms are better understood. Deep networks, on the other side, are very "black box" in that scientists do not completely understand the "inner" of deep networks. Because of the lack of a theoretical basis, hyperparameters and network design are also a challenge.

Here we have tried to give a detailed description of what makes deep learning stand out when compared with general Machine Learning. Let's go further in this learning journey and introduce you to the tool we will be using to practice deep learning in this book.

The Keras Deep Learning Framework

Now we've gone through deep learning foundations, let's dive into this book's main purpose: introduce you to deep learning using Python. In this book, a famous library called Keras, developed by Francois Chollet, will be the python deep learning library to be used here. Keras is very big, which implies that it does a lot of job for us so we can concentrate more on deep learning than on learning the tool. This section and subsequent chapters should be rather simple with the knowledge provided by previous chapters. But if you have questions or issues implementing the code that will be used in this book, the online community of Python deep learning is booming with passionate professionals who are always ready and ready to assist. This blog post lists various forums where you can get assistance on a trip comparable to yours and meet with others.

We will start with tiny networks with acceptable accuracies in this book, which will serve primarily as an insight into how Keras is used.

We will then offer an illustration of a more robust neural network that will use most of the above-described ideas. But first of all, let's look at the deep learning structure that we're going to use in the book: Keras.

A Deep Dive Into Keras

All our code instances will use Keras throughout the rest of this book. The Keras frame is a deep learning python frame designed to provide a fairly easy way to define and train just about any type of deep learning model. To enable fast experimentation, Keras was originally created for scientists.

- It allows to run smoothly on both GPU or CPU, basically the same code or really near.
- Keras is a very user-friendly API which makes simulating deep learning versions comparatively easy.
- It comes with built-in assistance for convolutional networks, when using with computer vision, recurring neural networks

(for chain processing), and a kind of combination of them both.

- Keras tends to help a lot of random network architectures like multi-input, multi-output, coating, version sharing, and more. This is proof that Keras does the work of building any type of deep learning model, ranging from generative adversarial networks to the construction of a Turing neural machine

The Keras framework is distributed under the permissive MIT license, which means it is offered to be freely utilized even in commercial endeavors. Keras is compatible with any version of Python installed on your system of choice, from Python 2.7 to 3.7 as of mid-2019.

Keras has far above 200,000 active users, and these users range from academic researchers and engineers at both startups and large companies to graduate students and amateurs. The Keras framework is put to use at giant impactful institutions such as Google, CERN, Uber, Netflix, Yelp, Square, and lots of other startups aimed at tackling a wide range of problems with varying degrees of difficulty and utility. Keras is also a popular framework used by competitors on Kaggle, a machine learning competition site, where a large percentage of every recent deep learning competition has been won by teams making use of the Keras deep learning framework.

An Introductory Keras Example

From this moment on we will use some Keras code, so it is correct to offer a detailed overview of what the Keras environment is like. This instance aims to show the strategy taken by Keras to the resolution of deep learning projects step by step. As mentioned previously, it is a very easy context to learn and I hope that this instance will demonstrate how true it is. Again, you have to type in the code and not simply read it, in order to gain a deep understanding of the workflow of Keras.

There isn't much code needed, but we'll step over it slowly so in the future you can generate your own models.

In this tutorial, the steps you will cover are:

- Load Data.
- Specify the model of Keras.
- Keras Model compilation.
- Model fit for Keras.
- Assess the model for Keras.
- Tie All together.

Once again, verify that you meet the following criteria to follow this example:

- Installation and configuration of Python 2 or 3.
- You installed and configured SciPy (which also includes NumPy).
- You've mounted and configured Keras and a backend (Theano or TensorFlow).

Create a fresh Python or Jupyter notebook file and type or copy and paste the code to the file.

1. Loading the Data

The first step is to identify the features and classes to be used.

We will load our data set using the NumPy library and use two Keras library courses to describe our template.

The necessary imports are shown below.

```
# instantiate keras neural network
from numpy import loadtxt
from keras.models import Sequential
from keras.layers import Dense
```

We can go ahead and load our dataset.

In this example, we are going to make use of the Pima Indian dataset for diabetes from the UCI machine learning database. This is a dataset containing medical records that identify if the diabetes occurred over a period of five years and whether it got added to the Pima Indians database.

The binary classification for diabetes is simple – 1 for yes, 0 for no. The input variables used for describing patients are all numeric and this means that using a neural network with numeric input and output values is much easier and is, in fact, the best place to start our Keras network.

We can get the data we require from:
- Dataset CSV File
- Dataset Details

Open both URLs, download the files and save them to your local working directory, where you installed Python. We are going to retain the name of pima-dataset.csv for the file.

Take a quick look inside the file and you will see a several rows of numbers that we are going to load as a matrix. To do this, we use a NumPy function called loadtxt(). The file contains eight input variables and a single output variable. The idea is to have our model learn how to map the rows of the input variables, identified as X, to the output variable identified as y, i.e. $y = f(X)$.

We can summarize the variables like this:

The input variables (x-axis) are:
1. Age in years
2. Type of diabetes
3. Patient BMI
4. mu U/ml – 2-hour serum
5. Skinfold thickness in mm – triceps
6. mm/Hg – diastolic blood pressure
7. Whether patient has been pregnant and how many times
8. Patient's blood glucose concentration

The output variables (y-axis) are:

1. A class variable with a value of either 0 or 1

Once you have loaded the CSV file into memory, we can split the information columns down into the input variables and the output variables. A 2D array is used for storing the training information – the first dimension is the rows and the second dimension is the columns.

To select two rows as a set, use the slice operator from NumPy or highlight the first 8 columns, from 0:8, and choose Select Sub-set Rows from 0:8.

```
# load dataset
data = loadtxt('pima-datasets.csv', delimiter=',')
# split into X and y axis (input/output variables)
X = data[:,0:8]
y = data[:,8]
```

We are now ready to configure our first neural network.

Keep in mind that we are working with a dataset containing nine columns so, if you use the range of 0:8, columns 0 through 7 are selected (remember, indexing begins at 0 not 1).

2. Configuring the Keras Model

In Keras, our models are generally configured into a sequence of layers.

We generate a Sequential model and incorporate layers simultaneously until we are happy about our model architecture.

The first thing to do is to guarantee that the input has the correct amount of input functionality. The first layer with the input dim discussion can be defined and set to 8 for the 8 inputs.

How do we understand the amount and shape of the layers?

It's a tough business. In the test and error testing procedure we use heuristics and often discover the most suited network arrangements (I shall attempt to convey this later). Usually, to capture the issue, you need a large network.

In this case we use a network structure with three layers, which is completely connected.

The Dense class defines completely linked layers. The first argument is to identify the number of cells or nodes in the layer and the activation function with the active argument.

Over the first 2 layers and from the output layer we use the rectified linear unit activation function known as ReLU.

In the past the activation functionality of Sigmoid and Tanh was a thumb rule for all layers, but in these days the ReLU activation function usually tends to produce improved results.

We use a sigmoid function on the output to ensure that the value of our network output is 0 to 1 and can easily be mapped to a Class 1 probability or snaps easily with a predictive limit of 0.5 for each class.

We can map it all together by incorporating each layer:
- Our model expects rows of data with eight input variables (that input_dim=8 part)
- The first of these hidden layers has 12 nodes and seems to make use of the ReLU activation function.
- The second hidden layer in this model seems to have 8 nodes and also makes use of the ReLU activation function.
- The output layer has one node and makes use of the sigmoid activation function.

```
# define your Keras model
model = Sequential()
model.add(Dense(12, input_dim=8, activation='relu'))
model.add(Dense(8, activation='relu'))
model.add(Dense(1, activation='sigmoid'))
```

Note that the sort of input in the design is deemed to be the first hidden layer debate. That's the most confusing thing. This means that the visible or input level and the first oversized layer in the code lines, adding the initial dense coating, are generally indicated for both these items.

3. Compiling our Keras Model

We can now compile the model since it has been configured.

The compilation of this model makes use of the numerically effective libraries that are included below such covers as Theano or TensorFlow (called 'the backend'). The backend selects the best way to depict the training and prediction network, for example with CPU or GPU, and also with distributed hardware.

During the network training, certain additional functions have to be indicated. Remember network training in order to find the best weight in our data set to map output inputs.

We need to identify the loss function, use the optimizer to scan the different weights and optional metrics for which we want to find them and report them during exercise, in order to evaluate the weight.

Cross-entropy will be the loss function we are going to employ in solving this problem. This loss function (Cross entropy) comes pre-installed in Keras as a binary_crossentropy and is used for problems that have to do with binary classification.

The optimizer to be used here will be defined as the effective algorithm 'Adam' optimizer on a stochastic gradient. This is a common variant of the gradient descent, as it tunes itself and outcomes in a variety of issues automatically.

Finally, we will retrieve and report the precision of the classification defined by the metric argument, because this is a classification problem.

compile your keras model

model.compile(loss='binary_crossentropy', optimizer='adam', metrics=['accuracy'])

4. Fitting our Keras Model

Our models were outlined and ready for efficient calculation. Now is the time for the model to operate on the given data.

We can train or adjust our model to our loaded data by calling fit() on the model. Training is carried out over time and is divided into lots each time.

- **Epoch**: The number of times that all rows of the training dataset will be passed through the model.
- **Batch**: At least one sample that the model should consider in an epoch before updating the weights.

One era includes one or more batches depending on the selected batch size (which is one of the parameters to be chosen when configuring your model), and the model is suitable for numerous periods.

The training method will operate throughout the data set of epochs for certain phases, which must be defined using arguing epochs. Before updating model weights in each age, we also need to set a few lines of data sets, call batch sizes and set them with a batch size argument.

We have a relatively small number of 10 for a small number of periods in this problem. This means that every moment (150/10), there are 15 model weight updates included.

These parameters can be picked by experimental testing and error selection. By training the model, we want the information lines to be mapped to the output score (or good enough). The model always has a bug, but after a certain stage of a particular model the number of an error rate will be set. This is known as the convergence model.

```
# fit Keras model on dataset
model.fit(X, y, epochs=150, batch_size=10)
Work on your GPU or your CPU takes place at this point
```

5. Evaluating our Keras Model

Our network was taught throughout the data set and that same dataset allows us to evaluate network performance.

This gives us a useful glimpse of how good a job we have done modeling the data (for example, the accuracy of the train), but not how smoothly the algorithm can operate with new data. You can divide your information into training data sets and test data sets preferably for the training and consequent evaluation of our models. With your teaching information set with the evaluate() method in our model, we can evaluate and transmit the exact same input data and output data used in the training of our model.

The outcomes, including the mean loss and other configured measures, are then collected and predicted such as the accuracy of each input and output pair. A list of two values will be returned with the evaluate() function. The first is the loss metric of the data set model and the next is the precision of the dataset model. The precision is only to be reported, so we disregard the importance of the loss.

```
# evaluate Keras model
_, accuracy = model.evaluate(X, y)
print('Accuracy: %.2f' % (accuracy*100))
```

6. As you have seen, creating neural networks with Keras is quite simple. The results of this network should show a loss and accuracy of 150 per epoch followed by the final evaluation. The ideal result is 1.0 accuracy and zero loss but the only time this is possible is when it is a trivial learning problem. The goal is to choose the best training settings and the best arrangement for the dataset you are using on order to get the maximum accuracy and the least loss.

If you are using an iPython or Jupyter notebook for this, be prepared to see several errors and this is down to progress bars. We can deactivate these as 0 by setting the value and the call features of the fit() function like this:

```
# Fit neural network with no progress bars
model.fit(X, y, epochs=150, batch_size=10, verbose=0)
# evaluate Keras model
_, accuracy = model.evaluate(X, y, verbose=0)
```

Keep in mind that your model's precision is different. The neural networks form a stochastic algorithm; this means that we can use the algorithm to train different models ever time the code is run using the same data. This is not a big in the system; it is a feature.

The changes in model output may require adjustments several times and then the average accuracy outcomes are calculated to ensure that your model performs fairly.

7. Testing our model with actual predictions

Newcomers to machine training often tend to ask this question: Now that I'm done with the training of my model, how do I predict fresh data? A fantastic issue. We can change the example above and predict the training information set by pretending that it is an unprecedented fresh data set.

Predicting is as simple as applying the predict() model function. In order to make predictions on problems in which our output lies between 0 and 1 we make use of the sigmoid activation feature on the output layer. After we're done with all that, our model can readily be transformed into a stable binary projection for this classification problem.

```
# make probability predictions using the model
predictions = model.predict(X)
# round predictions
rounded = [round(x[0]) for x in predictions]
```

Otherwise, on our Keras model, predict_classes() may be called to directly predict different classes, like this:

make predictions with your Keras model

predictions = model.predict_classes(X)

A Summary Of Our Keras Model

In the course of this example, we have shown how to use the amazing Keras Python library to build your first neural network model.

In the course of this example, we have shown the six main measures to employ while building a neural network step-by-step with the help of Keras:

- Loading data into a Keras neural network.

- Processes involved in setting up a neural Keras network.

- The steps involved in the building of a Keras model using the powerful numerical backend.

- We have shown the training of a Keras model on data.

- We've illustrated the steps involved in evaluating a model on data.

- We tested our model by making predictions.

The Internet Movie Database (IMDB)

In this dataset, we have exactly twenty-five thousand reviews that make up the test set and another twenty-five thousand reviews that make up our validation set. The test set and validation set are further divided, half to contain positive reviews, and the other half contains positive reviews. Therefore, you will work with exactly fifty thousand extremely polarized Internet Movie Database Reviews in this dataset.

One might ask why exactly we are making use of separate training sets and test sets. The reason for this is that in order to get a well-generalized machine learning model, you should never use the data you used to train your model as your validation dataset. Since the model has already encountered that dataset, it can give very high percentage accuracies, tricking you into thinking that the model works properly but in reality, it only memorized what the output to every input it had encountered was. Therefore, when this model encounters data that it has never seen, it tends to perform rather poorly; and the efficiency of the model with new data is what you are concerned with. This is highly ineffective when trying to predict the data targets never seen before in the model. In the next chapters we will go see how exactly this works.

The dataset IMDB is already mounted in Keras, as we have seen with the MNIST data set. Checks (word sequences) must be depicted as a set of components, each of which must be a specific word in a dictionary. In order to render this region totally unnecessary, the details were prepared and cleaned. The following codes load the data (data is saved at the first point of the configuration or loading of your personal computer, which uses approximately 80 MB).

How the IMDB dataset is loaded into our Keras model
from keras.datasets import imdb
(train_data, train_labels), (test_data, test_labels) = imdb.load_data(
num_words=10000)

The num_words=10000 reasoning implies that you will only maintain in the training data the highest of 10,000 words. Rare words are going to be rejected. This enables you to operate with manageable vector data. The train data and test data variables are the checklists; each evaluation is a word index list (word sequence encoding). The arguments train_labels and test_labels are lists that contain values of either 0 or 1. In this case, whenever the value is 0 that represents a negative review, and conversely, a 1 represents a positive review:

```
>>> train_data[0]
[1, 14, 22, 16, ... 178, 32]
>>> train_labels[0]
1
```

As you limit yourself to the top 10,000 most common phrases, no word index exceeds 10,000:

```
>>> max([max(sequence) for sequence in train_data])
9999
```

If you are interested in knowing how to get these reviews back to English, here's how you could do that:

word_index = imdb.get_word_index()

reverse_word_index = dict([(value, key) for (key, value) in word_index.items()])

decoded_review = ' '.join(

[reverse_word_index.get(i - 3, '?') for i in train_data[0]])

- It is not feasible to add entire lists to a neural network. Your lists need to be turned into tensors. There are two methods for managing a tensor integral (the embedding level we will discuss in a book later on) by placing your list in a tensor form (samples, word indicators). It's the first layer of your network.

- List should be one hot encoded to convert it to 0 and 1 vectors. For example, this means converting the sequence[3,5] into 10,000-dimensional vectors, all 0s, with the exception of three and five indicators.

- You can then use the first layer of your network as a dense layer, which can manage the floating-point vector information.

We will take the latter approach, which you will do manually to ensure as much transparency as possible.

Encoding of an integer sequence in a binary matrix:

import numpy as np

```
def vectorize_sequences(sequences, dimension=10000):
    results = np.zeros((len(sequences), dimension))
    for i, sequence in enumerate(sequences):
        results[i, sequence] = 1. # Sets specific indices return results of
results[i]  to 1s
x_train = vectorize_sequences(train_data) #Vectorized training data
x_test = vectorize_sequences(test_data) # Vectorized test data
```

The sample is then transformed to look like this:
```
>>> x_train[0]
array([ 0., 1., 1., ..., 0., 0., 0.])
```

The next step will then be to vectorize our labels. This is a rather simple process when you use Keras:
```
y_train = np.asarray(train_labels).astype('float32')
y_test = np.asarray(test_labels).astype('float32')
```
Now the data is ready to be fed into a neural network.

Configuring Your Neural Network

Vectors and scalars (1s and 0s) are the data inputs: this is your easiest setup to achieve. A well-functioning network form for such a problem is a simple stack of fully connected (Dense) layers, with re-activation: dense(16), active(='relu') The argument for each layer of dense(16) is the number of units in the cloak. A concealed device is a dimension in the screen room layer.

If there are 16 concealed units then the weight of the matrix W is formed (input dimension, 16). Thus, the input data of W is shown onto the vector b and the ReLU in a sixteen-dimensional display space. The objective is "how much liberty do you give to the network when you study inner officials" in an intuitive way, and your network can learn more complex images with other hidden components (higher representation space).

A stack of densely constructed layers has two major architectural choices to be made or questions to be answered:

- What number of layers should be used?

- Within each layer, what number of hidden layers should be used?

You will learn formal values with adequate and concentrated exercise to guide you in these decisions. For now, I will design my neural network using the following architecture:

- Two mid-layers each with 16 hidden units

- A third level which gives a scalar forecast of the accuracy of the present assessment

The middle layers are activated by ReLU, and the final layer is activated by sigmoid to give a probability (score between 0 and 1 indicating the probability that the sample will be targeted "1": how positive the test may be). A ReLU (linear unit rectified) is a feature that has the effect of zero adverse values, while an arbitrary[0, 1] sigmoid "squashes" values that are likely to be interpreted as a probability.

Defining our Model

```
from keras import models
from keras import layers
model = models.Sequential()
model.add(layers.Dense(16, activation='relu',
input_shape=(10000,)))
model.add(layers.Dense(16, activation='relu'))
model.add(layers.Dense(1, activation='sigmoid'))
```

You may be asking yourself what exactly the activation functions are, and what purpose they really serve. The dense layer consists of two linear activities-a dot product and a supplement-without the activation function ReLU (also called a nonlinearity) expressed as: output = dot(W, input) + b

This enables the layer to learn only a linear conversion (refined transformations) of the input data: the layer's hypothesis room would be a collection of feasible linear input data transitions into a 16-dimensional space. The hypothesis is too tiny to accommodate several layers as it is still possible to conduct a linear operation in a deep linear layer stack: adding additional layers would not stretch the room for the hypothesis.

You need a non-linear activation function in order to access a very wealthy room that benefits from deep representation. ReLU is the primary activating feature of deep education, but has many other applicants with likewise unusual names, including PReLU, eLU, etc. Finally, a loss feature and an optimizer must be selected.

Because a problem can be resolved in binary classification and you expect the network to be likely (because the sigmoidal activation on the neural layer of your neural unit has ended), binary_crossentropy is the most effective loss characteristic. This is definitely not the only feasible option: for example, the mean squared error (MSE) could be used. However, when you deal with model outcomes, cross-entropy is generally the best choice. Cross entropy is an information theory quantity measuring the distance between the distribution of probabilities or, in this instance, the distribution of ground truth and your forecasts.

This is the step to configure the model with the rmsprop optimizer and the loss function for binary cross-entropy. Please note that during training, you will also check for precision.

Compiling Our Model

```
model.compile(optimizer='rmsprop',
loss='binary_crossentropy',
metrics=['accuracy'])
```

Using Keras, our parameters (which are the optimizer, loss function, and metrics) which will be passed into our neural network as strings, and this is because Keras comes prepackaged with rmsprop, binary_crossentropy, and accuracy which makes our work a bit easier, as is the aim of the Keras framework.

You can sometimes configure or pass a custom loss or metric function to set your optimizer parameters. The latter could take place through the passing of functional objects as loss and/or metrics argument as shown above by passing an optimizer class example as the optimizer argument.

Next, we place our chosen optimizer into our Keras model
from keras import optimizers
model.compile(optimizer=optimizers.RMSprop(lr=0.001),
loss='binary_crossentropy',
metrics=['accuracy'])
Though you can also make use of custom losses and metrics like so:
from keras import losses
from keras import metrics
model.compile(optimizer=optimizers.RMSprop(lr=0.001),
loss=losses.binary_crossentropy,
metrics=[metrics.binary_accuracy])

Validating Your Approach

You generate a validation set by selecting 10,000 samples from the initial workout information in order to monitor the precision of the model over training data you have never seen before.

Keeping a part of the dataset to be used to validate the network
x_val = x_train[:10000]
partial_x_train = x_train[10000:]
y_val = y_train[:10000]
partial_y_train = y_train[10000:]

At this point in 20 epochs, we are continuing the training of the model into mini-packs of 512 samples (20 iterations for all x train and y train samples). You can simultaneously monitor loss and accuracy in the 10,000 samples you separate. By transmitting validation data as a validation data argument.

Let's train our model
```
model.compile(optimizer='rmsprop',
loss='binary_crossentropy',
metrics=['acc'])
history = model.fit(partial_x_train,
partial_y_train,
epochs=20,
batch_size=512,
validation_data=(x_val, y_val))
```

Training on the CPU is 20 seconds away. It requires under 2 seconds per epoch. The model calculates its loss and precision by the 10,000 validation information samples at the end of each period, a tiny break happens.

Please note the History item is returned with a call to model.fit(). This returns an object that contains the history attribute, which is basically a dictionary containing information on all training sessions. Let us have a look at it:

```
>>> history_dict = history.history
>>> history_dict.keys()
[u'acc', u'loss', u'val_acc', u'val_loss']
```

There are four entries in the dictionary: 1 per metric monitored during exercise and validation. In the following code snippet, we will use Matplotlib to monitor training, validation and precise training and validation loss on the side. Be aware that your own results can vary somewhat but are only slightly due to a further random initialization of your network.

Visualizing our training and validation loss

```
import matplotlib.pyplot as plt

history_dict = history.history
loss_values = history_dict['loss']
val_loss_values = history_dict['val_loss']

epochs = range(1, len(acc) + 1)

plt.plot(epochs, loss_values, 'bo', label='Training loss')
plt.plot(epochs, val_loss_values, 'b', label='Validation loss')
plt.title('Training and validation loss')
plt.xlabel('Epochs')
blue line."
plt.ylabel('Loss')
plt.legend()

plt.show()
```

As you can see, the loss of training falls at all stages and the precision of training increases at each level. This is what you'd expect from the optimization of the gradient descent–the amount you want with each iteration should be less. The loss of precision and validation is not the case; the fourth phase appears to be highly significant. This is an instance of what we have warned about: a better data education model is not necessarily a better information model that was never previously seen. In concrete terms what you see is excessive: the training information is over-optimized after the second phase and you end up with pictures that are specific to the formation information and that do not generalize to statistics outside the formation.

In this scenario, after three epochs, you can stop training to prevent overfitting. In general, you can use a number of techniques to decrease overcasting later on.

Deep Learning for Images

This chapter will introduce the concept of neural convolutional networks, also known as neural neurons. Convenient neural networks are currently highly successful and deeply efficient, particularly for images of excellent significance to autonomous scientists who do not have access to large resources. In particular, pictures in small training datasets can be discovered.

An Introduction To The Concept Of The Convolutional Neural Network

We're about to learn theory what convolutional neural networks are and why the computer vision activities were so effective. First of all, let's look at a straightforward neural network instance, in practical terms. It allows use for MNIST numbers through a convolutional neural network, a job we did previously with a densely linked network in this book (then our test precision was 97.8%). Although the convolutional neural network is essential, the precision of the previous shorter models will blow this one out of the water.

The following code lines are aimed at demonstrating to you what a fundamental neural network looks. It is a pile of layers Conv2D and MaxPooling2D. Exactly what they do, I'll try to make clear in a minute.

```
# Instantiate a small convolutional neural network
from keras import layers
from keras import models
model = models.Sequential()
model.add(layers.Conv2D(32, (3, 3), activation='relu',
input_shape=(28, 28, 1)))
model.add(layers.MaxPooling2D((2, 2)))
model.add(layers.Conv2D(64, (3, 3), activation='relu'))
model.add(layers.MaxPooling2D((2, 2)))
model.add(layers.Conv2D(64, (3, 3), activation='relu'))
```

Importantly, input tensors for form (image height, image width, image channels), including the batch dimension, are used in a convolutional neural network. In this case the convolutional neural network can also be configured for processing size inputs (28, 28, 1), the MNIST images format. This can be done by passing the input_shape=(28, 28, 1) argument to the first layer.

As you can see, each MaxPooling 2D and Conv2D layer has an output of 3D Tensing – height, broadness, channels. The deeper the network goes, the more you will see the height and width dimensions decrease. The first parameter or argument for the Conv2D layers is used for controlling how many channels there are.

Next, a tightly linked classifier network is added to the final output tensor, with a shape of (3, 3, 64). This type of classifier processes 1D vectors – we already know that we have a 3D tensor as the current output. In the first case, we should apply the 3D outputs with 1D and then add a few more dense layers:

```
model.add(layers.Flatten())
model.add(layers.Dense(64, activation='relu'))
model.add(layers.Dense(10, activation='softmax'))
```

We can now use our final layer for 10-way classification problems because it has softmax activation and 10 inputs.

Before the (3, 3, 64) output is passed through a pair of dense layers, it gets reshaped to a shape vector (576). When the MNIST numbers are trained on your CNN, the tightly-linked network will have a

99.3% test precision – this is good, the relative error rate has been reduced by 68%.

The one questions you should be asking is, how can such a simple network work as well as it does as a tightly linked classifier model? To answer that, we need to look at how the MaxPooling 2D and Conv2D layers work.

What Is The Convolution Operation?

Dense layers are designed in the input function to learn global patterns (like in the patterns found in digits of MNIST, patterns of all the pixels), while in the case of the patterns on the small 2D windows of inserts, the convolutional layers are designed to recognize local patterns. The primary difference between a closely associated layer and a level of convolution is that these windows were in the previous 3 to 3.

Photos can be broken into patterns such as corners, textures and so on. This major characteristic provides the neural convolutional networks two interesting features:

Invariant in the patterns you learn, this translation. In the bottom correct corner of a picture, a convolutional neural network can recognize a pattern, for example in the left top corner. If it came to a new location, the pattern should again be known to a strongly connected network. This efficient image data treatment (since the visual environment is mainly invariant in translation) makes convolutional neural networks efficient: fewer training samples are needed to know how to generalize representation.

They are able to recognize spatial pattern hierarchies. A first overlay captured tiny local patterns, like borders, a second overlay captured bigger patterns of first layer characteristics etc. This enables convolutional neural networks to learn more and more complicated and abstract visual ideas effectively (because the visual environment is basically hierarchical).

The visual environment forms a range of visual components: hyperlocal rims merge with local objects such as eyes or ears which mix into high-level conceptuals such as "cat." Convolutions operate on 3D tensors with the two space axes (height and width) and also the axis of depth referred to in the name of the function map (also known as the channel axis). The depth of the axis of the image with RGB amounts to 3, since the image is made of 3 colors: red, green and blue. The depth is 1 (gray levels)/. The convolution function extracts patches from its input character map and transforms all these patches in the same way and creates the output characteristic map. This output characteristic map is still a 3D tensor: its width and height are present. Its thickness can be arbitrary as output profile is a layer parameter, and the various channels in that thickness axis are no longer for particular colors like in RGB input; rather, they are filters. Filters encode certain elements of the input data: for example, the concept "facial presence in the input" could be encoded at a high level with one filter.

The first convolution layer, when looking at an MNIST instance, uses a size characteristic map (28, 28, 1) and produces a size characteristic map (2, 26, 26, 32): it calculates 32 filters over the input. Every single one of these 32 output channels is a grid of 26 to 26 values that represents a reaction map of the filter over the input that shows the filter pattern reaction at separate input places. That is the meaning of the function map: the 2D tensor output[:,:,n] is the 2D spatial map of the filter's reaction over the input, and every element in the depth axis is a function (or filter) map of response, quantification of the pattern appearance of the filter at various sites. The idea of an answer map: a 2D map of how a pattern is present at various places in an entrance. Two main parameters define these configurations:

- Patch size obtained from the inputs — Typically 3 paragraphs are 3 or 5 paragraphs 5. The instance shows that they were 3 to 3, a common choice.

- Depth of the output function — Number of convolution-calculated filters. The example that is shown here began on 32 deep and finished on 64 deep.

When dealing with Keras convolutional (Conv2D) layers, the most frequently used method is to first of all pass these arguments into the layer like so: Conv2D(output_depth, (window_height, window_width)).

The way the convolutional operation is invoked is by passing these windows of shape 3 × 3 or of shape 5 × 5 over the 3D input feature map, while taking care to stop and extract a 3D patch of surrounding features at every possible location (resulting in shape (window_height, window_width, input_depth)). Every one of these 3D patches is then passed through a transformation process. Every one of these individual vectors is further manipulated and spatially rearranged into a 3D output map which has the shape of (height, width, output_depth). The space in the output function map corresponds to the same position on the input function map (e.g. the bottom right corner of the output includes information on the bottom right corner of the induction). For example, when given a window of dimension 3 × 3, what seems to come from the 3D patch input[i-1:i+1, j-1:j+1, :] is the vector output[i, j, :] .

How Convolution Works

Note that the width and height of the input and height may differ. For two reasons, they may vary. The first is because of the effect of borders, which can usually be countered by padding the input function map. The second reason is because of the use of steps which will be defined in a short time.

Let's look into these concepts more deeply.

Understanding The Concept of Border Effects And Padding

If a five by five tile is available (which means a total of 25tiles). Only 9tyles appear to be accessible to center a three by three window to create a three by three grid that can mentally be photographed. Therefore, the output characteristic map will be three by three. It tends to decrease a little: exactly by two tiles next to each aspect in this scenario. This limiting effect can be seen in practice in the previous instance: you start with 28 by 28tiles that become a 26 by 26 layer after the first convolution.

You can use padding if you need an output function map with the same range as the input. The padding comprises of adding a specific amount of rows and columns to each side of the input map so that the convolution Windows can be fitted around each input sheet. If it happens to be a window of dimension three by three window, in such a case it will make sense to add a single column on the right, another on the left, one row appended to the top, and yet another row appended at the bottom. For a five by five sized window, two rows need to be added, and so on and so forth.

In convolutional layers on the other hand, we can always adjust the padding by simply making use of the argument 'padding', which is configured with one of two values: "valid" string that means no padding (only windows are valid); and the string "same" that means "padding with a power output of the same width and height as the input." "similar" string means "pad" The default value of the padding argument is "valid".

Understanding The Concept of Convolutional Slides
One important factor that is capable of influencing the output size vital concept of convolutional slides. The convolution description has supposed to this point, that the central tiles on the convergence windows are all in some way, adjoining. However, the gap between two consecutive windows is a convolution parameter called the step

that defaults to 1. Strong convolutions can occur; convolutions with a step above 1. The patches obtained by a three-to-three convolution with step 2 over 5x5 of the input (not packed).

Step 2 implies that, in relation to any modifications induces by the boundary impacts, the width and height of the map are sampled by a factor 2. In practice, strided convolutions are seldom used, though some models are useful; the idea is nice to know.

We tend to use a max-pooling procedure, which you saw in the first neural network instance to show function maps instead of steps. Let's take a closer look at it.

Introducing The Concept Of Max Pooling

In the example introduced by the neural network, you may have found that, after every MaxPooling2D layer, the size of the maps is halved. The function map for instance is 26 x 26 before the first MaxPooling2D concentrations, but it is halved to 13 x 13 by the max-pooling procedure.

That is the role of max pooling, like strided convolutions to aggressively downsample function maps.

Instead of learning linear transformation, the Max pooling is the extraction of windows from the maps of input and the output of each channel's highest value (the co-convolution), except that local patches are transformed with a hard-coded, maximum tensor action. A large distinction is the fact that max-pooling is generally performed with 2x 2 windows and step 2 to sample the

91

characteristic maps with a factor of 2. Converting is usually carried out with 3 to 3 windows and no step (stride 1), on the other side.

Why this is the case for downsampling maps? How can we not remove the max-pooling layers and maintain relatively big function maps? Let's take this choice into account. This would look like the convolutional foundation of the model:

```
model_no_max_pool = models.Sequential()
model_no_max_pool.add(layers.Conv2D(32, (3, 3), activation='relu',
input_shape=(28, 28, 1)))
model_no_max_pool.add(layers.Conv2D(64, (3, 3), activation='relu'))
model_no_max_pool.add(layers.Conv2D(64, (3, 3), activation='relu'))
Let's print out the summary of our model:
>>> model_no_max_pool.summary()
Layer (type)
```

What's wrong with this system? Two things: it isn't helpful to learn that an attribute hierarchy. In the next layer of 3x3 windows, data from 7 to 7 windows from the first entry will be included. However, in terms of the initial input signal, which might be not enough to know how to classify chords (merely considering the figure by using windows of about seven to seven pixels) high-tech patterns listened to by the convolutional neural networks are very low. We want to include information about the totality of this input signal in the characteristics from the past overlay. That's huge. If a dense layer of dimension 512 should be attached to the top, this coating could be 15.8 million. For such a small model, this is far too large and could result in extreme overfitting. In simple words, it appears at large windows as to the part they pay for their first entry that the reasons for the use of down spectrum are to reduce the number of functional map coefficients to the procedure, and to trigger space filter hierarchies through the creation of consecutive overlay layers. Notice that you cannot achieve such downsampling by peak pooling alone. As you understand, in the past convolution layer you might even use steps.

Instead of maximum pooling, you can use an average pool where every neighborhood input is altered by taking each station in the patch's average value as opposed to the max. However, peak pooling will operate better than alternatives. The rationale for this is that characteristics are likely to encode the spatial presence of a pattern or theory over different tiles of this characteristic map (thus, the term characteristic map), so the maximum existence of separate characteristics rather than their typical presence is more informative.

Therefore, the very sensible strategy is to create thick maps of characteristics (with undistorted convolutions) and then examine the peak activation of qualities over small patches rather than taking account of smaller windows of these outputs (with steep convolutions) or the average input stains. You now have to know how to build a small convolutional neural network to tackle a toy problem like MNIST digit classifications — maps, convolutions and peak grouping. They also need to know how to build a little convolutional neural network.

For the identification of numbers using MNIST data set we will be using a 5-layer linear neural network. The machine learning problem that has been known for a long time as the ABC of computer vision is the MNIST data set. The MNIST dataset is a collection of all the single digits (0 and 9) written by the human hand. These numbers are distorted in various ways, in a bid to closely mirror the way numbers are written by individuals in the real world. In this instance, we will attempt to offer you a full perspective of how deep learning issues can be resolved. We first clean/prepared information, then concentrate on modeling and evaluating the concurrent neural network and then go through the prediction and submission segment of outcomes.

For this example, it is recommended that the reader makes use of a Google Colab Jupyter Notebook because Google colab provides researchers with free GPUs.

CNNs can identify vital/useful features wherever they are found on these transformed images. These features identified are formed into things called 'feature maps'.

Another important layer in the CNN is known as the pooling or MaxPool2D layer. The pooling layer acts as a sieve. It takes a look at two neighboring pixels then takes the larger value between both. They are used mainly to drive down computational cost and also to reduce the chances of overfitting. Before using this, the pooling size has to be chosen. The greater the pooling size, the more the need to downsample.

Using both of these different types of layers (CNNs and pooling), our system is able to efficiently extract both the local and global patterns in the image.

In our system, we'll use 'dropouts'. The Dropout is a technique used to regularization where portions of the nodes in a layer are ignored randomly. This drops a portion of the network then forces it to learn patterns in a distributed fashion. This tends to help make a system more capable of generalizing, thereby reducing overfitting.

The code contains a section in which we define an "activation" keyword argument as "relu." Deep learning activation functions are a very significant element in defining artificial neural networks. They are used to decide whether or not a node should be activated. It decides if the information received by the node should be utilized or ignored.

The 'relu' is a rectifier. It is an activation function which is used to add nonlinearity to a neural network. It basically checks if a value being passed is greater than zero and can thus be written as $f(x) = max(0, x)$. Relu is very effective and is thus very popular in deep learning. Why is such a simple function so effective in adding nonlinearity to our models?

Flattens are used to collapse the final feature maps into single 1D vectors. This flattening process combines all the local features that were discovered by the previous convolutional layers. This is needed so as to be able to use fully connected layers after using convolutional and max-pool layers.

Setting Our Optimizer

While planning out the architecture of our model, we need to make a few important choices. These include a loss function, score function and an optimization algorithm.

The essence of the loss function is to give an estimate of how poorly our model performs on the images contained in our training dataset (images which we know the 'correct' value for). This function represents the error rate between the observed labels and the predicted ones. We use a specific form for categorical classifications (>2 classes) called the categorical cross-entropy.

While the loss function is important, the most vital function you'll have to choose is called the optimizer. The optimizer tries to iteratively improve parameters such as the filters of kernel values, weights and the biases of neurons, etc. with the aim of reducing the loss to the minimum.

- In this example we'll be using RMSprop with its default values. RMSprop is a highly efficient optimizer that tweaks the AdaGrad method in an attempt to reduce its aggressive, monotonically learning rate. There is another optimizer which could be used called the Stochastic Gradient Descent ('sgd') optimizer, but it is a lot slower than RMSprop.

There are a few metrics which can be used to measure how well our model works. The "accuracy" metric is one of these. The accuracy metric function is somewhat similar to the loss function, except that the results from the metric evaluation are not used when training the model and are rather used for evaluation purposes only.

In [12]:
```
# Define optimizer
optimizer = RMSprop(lr=0.001, rho=0.9, epsilon=1e-08,
decay=0.0)
```

In [13]:
```
# Compile model
model.compile(optimizer = optimizer, loss =
"categorical_crossentropy", metrics=["accuracy"])
```

In the architecture of neural networks, one vital goal to aim for is the rapid and close convergence of the optimizer with the global minimum of the loss function. In our example, the annealing method of the learning rate (LR) is used to achieve this.

The rate of learning is the pace through the 'loss landscape' for optimizers. The larger the steps and the faster the convergence, the greater the learning rate. However, the sample rate is very poor, and the optimizer could likely be reduced to a minimum local level.

In the practice of machine learning a declining learning rate is usually better to achieve the global minimum loss function effectively during training.

I have dynamically decreased my learning rate every x-step (eight) to maintain the value of the fast computational time with the high learning rate depending on whether it's necessary (if precise).

Data Augmentation

We need to artificially expand our handwritten digit dataset in order to prevent overfitting problems. We can even enlarge your current dataset. The concept is to change training data with tiny transformations so that the changes occur when someone writes a digit are reproduced.

The scale is not the same (some who write big and small numbers), for example, and the image is rotated. The number is not centered.

An approach, known as information augmentation methods, alters the training information in ways which modify the table representation while maintaining the label. Some common increases are gray scales, horizontal flips, vertical flips, random plants, chat colors, translations, rotations, and more.

By using only a few of these transitions in our training information, the amount of training examples is easy to double or triple and we can generate a strong model.

The changes this makes is immediately obvious: Without applying the method of data augmentation, we were able to hit a rate of accuracy of 98.114% but when data augmentation was applied, we got an accuracy rate of 99.67% of accuracy

Applying the important technique of data augmentation to our example required my doing a few things. First, I had to rotate random parts of images contained in our training dataset. Some parts of images contained in our training set were slightly zoomed in, by about ten percent. Some images were slightly shifted horizontally by about ten percent of the width of the image, and some images were slightly shifted vertically by about ten percent of the height of the image.

In the course of the training cycles I found that in order to not misclassify numbers that are symmetrical (symmetrical numbers such as 6 and 9) I'll have to remove the vertical_flip and horizontal_flip.

Once we are done with our model, we go on to fitting the training dataset.

The validation data set after 2 stages is validated with nearly 99 percent (98.7+ percent) precision. Almost every moment during training, the validation precision is higher than the training precision. So our model does not overfit the training set.

Introduction To The Concept Of The Confusion Matrix

The Confusion matrix is another amazing machine learning technique. It tends to be one very useful technique if you are interested in seeing where exactly the model you are training fails.

In this example, we visualize the confusion matrix for the validation set:

In [20]:

Visualize the confusion matrix

def plot_confusion_matrix(cm, classes,

```
                    normalize=False,
                    title='Confusion matrix',
                    cmap=plt.cm.Blues):
    """
    Function used to print the confusion matrix and plot it.
    Set 'normalize=True' to apply normalization,
    """
    plt.imshow(cm, interpolation='nearest', cmap=cmap)
    plt.title(title)
    plt.colorbar()
    tick_marks = np.arange(len(classes))
    plt.xticks(tick_marks, classes, rotation=45)
    plt.yticks(tick_marks, classes)

    if normalize:
        cm = cm.astype('float') / cm.sum(axis=1)[:, np.newaxis]

    thresh = cm.max() / 2.
    for  i,   j   in   itertools.product(range(cm.shape[0]),
range(cm.shape[1])):
        plt.text(j, i, cm[i, j],
                horizontalalignment="center",
                color="white" if cm[i, j] > thresh else "black")

    plt.tight_layout()
    plt.ylabel('True label')
    plt.xlabel('Predicted label')
```

```
# Predict the values from the validation dataset
Y_pred = model.predict(X_val)
# Convert predictions classes to one-hot vectors
Y_pred_classes = np.argmax(Y_pred,axis = 1)
# Convert validation observations to one-hot vectors
Y_true = np.argmax(Y_val,axis = 1)
# compute confusion matrix
confusion_mtx = confusion_matrix(Y_true, Y_pred_classes)
# plot confusion matrix
plot_confusion_matrix(confusion_mtx, classes = range(10))
```

From the code above it is obvious that our convolutional neural network is very precise and accurate when dealing with all digits that contain a few errors when compared with the size of the validation set (which consists of a total of about 4,200 images).

Our convolutional neural network, however, tends to have some glitches for example whenever it happens to encounter the '4' digit, it immediately classifies it as a '9'. In most cases, it can be a very tedious job to pick out the differences between numbers 4 and 9, especially written in such a way that curves are smooth.

We've gone through a thorough end to end example of the building of a highly performant convolutional neural network which can accurately predict handwritten digits. In this example, we went through all the stages involved in the typical deep learning project. We went from data mining to data preparation to thinking through the different parameters vital to the performance of our neural network architecture to iteratively improving the model to squeeze out as much accuracy as we can manage. While this model can be improved, the aim of this example was to give the reader a peek as to the step by step processes through which a lot of the mind-blowing machine learning products we know of and use, are actually created by practitioners.

We've explored the creation of an efficient image classifier. Other examples in this book will explore other fields of deep learning, and though they will not be as detailed as the above example, we will try to explain our thought process as to why we choose to use whatever technique we use. This of course is just an expose into the world of deep learning and is in no way meant as a definitive approach to attacking all deep learning problems, but should rather be viewed by readers as a springboard to understand and explore other even more efficient and advanced techniques which can be employed to squeeze even more accuracy and efficiency from their own deep learning models.

Now we are going to explore other applications of deep learning.

Deep Learning For Text Data

Text is probably the most frequently used form of sequence data. Text data can either be processed as a sequence of individual characters or it can be processed as a sequence of words, but the most common way of processing text is at the level of words. The following sequence-processing deep learning models we are going to introduce in the following sections will be trained to produce a high level natural-language understanding which can be applied in use cases such as question answering (Q&A) robots, document classification programs, sentiment analysis, author identification, etc. all by the use of sequenced text as input. To be clear, of all the deep learning models that will be used throughout this chapter, none actually *understand* the text as a human being will, rather these models try to map out the statistical structure of written language, which is often sufficient when aimed at solving a lot of simple textual problems. Deep learning when used for NLP can be viewed as pattern recognition as applied to sentences, words, and paragraphs the same way deep learning for images (or computer vision) can be viewed as pattern recognition as applied to image pixels.

It is important to remember that neural networks never take in data in their raw form, rather all data to be fed into a neural network has to be first converted into tensors/matrices. This 'vectorization' process as was called before will also be employed in dealing with text sequences. Vectorizing text refers to all the processes involved in the transformation of data received as text into tensors that are numeric. This transformation can be carried out in different ways: by trying to segment the text received into words, then transforming every word to a vector; by trying to segment the text received into characters, then transforming every character to a vector; by extracting n-grams of words and characters, then transforming every n-gram to a vector.

Together, the various units in which you'll be able to divide text (characters, words, and n-grams) are known as tokens, and dividing text to these tokens is known as tokenization. All the text-vectorization procedures consist of employing some tokenization plot and then linking numerical vectors using the created tokens. All these vectors, joined with chain tensors, are fed to deep learning systems. There are numerous methods to connect a vector using a token. The rest of this segment describes the techniques and shows how to utilize them to change the raw text into NumPy tensors which you are able to send to some Keras network.

Text
"Deep learning is the absolute best."
Tokens
"Deep", "learning", "is", "the", "absolute", "best", "."
Vector encoding of the tokens

Deep	learning	is	the absolute	best	.
0.0	0.0	0.4	0.0 0.0	1.0	0.0
0.5	1.5	0.5	0.20.5	0.5	0.0
1.0	0.2	1.0	1.01.0	0.0	0.0

Understanding N-Grams And Bag-Of-Words

Word n-grams are the successive N (or lesser) words you can extract from a phrase. Instead of words, it can also be used for characters. Here we will present a simple illustration of the concept of N-grams. Consider the sentence: "Deep learning is the absolute best." It may be decomposed into the following set of 2-grams:

{"Deep", "Deep learning", "learning", "learning is", "is", "is the", "the", "the absolute", "absolute", "absolute best", "best"}

The sentence can also be broken down into the following set of 3-grams:

{"Deep", "Deep learning", "learning", "learning is", "Deep learning is", "is", "is the", "the", "learning is the", "the absolute", "absolute", "is the absolute", "absolute best", "best", "the absolute best"}

A set of words in these sorts of sequences are called a bag-of-2-grams or bag-of-3-grams, respectively.

The term 'bag' here is really pointing to how you are to handle a couple of tokens rather than hinting at a sort of list or group: tokens are not arranged in any particular order. This technique of tokenization is referred to as a bag of words.

Since bag-of-words is not a tokenization method that is aimed at maintaining the order of objects, meaning that tokens that are generated are taken in as a set rather than a sequence, meaning that the overall linguistic structure of the sequence of words is totally discarded, the technique of bag-of-words is generally not used in deep learning language processing, but is better suited to more rather shallow language processing neural networks. N-graphs is a type of feature engineering, which is replaced with hierarchical feature training by deeper learning that removes this kind of rigid and brittle strategy. One-dimensional connotations and repetitive neural networks, introduced later in this section, are able, by constant word sequences and character sequence, to learn depictions from words and personalities, without being explicitly informed about their presence. That's why in this book we're not going to cover n-grams. But remember that when using lightweight, shallow text processing models such as logistic regression, and random forests, they are a strong, unavoidable feature-engineering instrument.

From Labels to One-Hot Encoding

An important part of machine learning is understanding a process called 'one-hot encoding'. Not the easiest for beginners to learn and you do need some knowledge of machine and deep learning so let me try to explain it as simply as I can.

When you build a machine learning model, the first thing you have to do is preprocess your data. That means, as you already know, the data needs to be prepared so your model can analyze it. You can't just chuck a load of data or images at your model and expect that it knows exactly what it is doing.

Encoding is a fundamental part of preprocessing; each bit of the data must be represented in such a way that the computer understands it – the term 'encode' quite literally translates to "convert to code". And there are loads of ways to encode data, with one label encoding and on-hot encoding being two of the most important. I'll start with label encoding as this gives you a better understanding of one-hot encoding.

Let's imagine that we have some categorical data to work with, cats and dogs for example. Label encoding is relatively straightforward – it encodes the labels which are nothing more than categories, such as cat and dog. All encoding does is gives each label a number that represents a particular category – we might, for example, encode cat as 1 and dog as 2. By doing this, the computer is now able to represent them because, after all, computers work with numbers.

That is label encoding in a nutshell, but it doesn't always work when you have categorical data. Why not? It's quite simple – label encoding gives the categories naturally ordered relationships – computers are programmed to treat a bigger number as just that and, naturally, the bigger the number, the bigger the weight. We can see how this works with a simple example:

Let's say that we three food categories – oranges, beef, cauliflower. With label encoding, each category would be given a number – oranges = 1, beef = 2, cauliflower = 3. Now, if your machine model needs to make an internal calculation of the average across the categories, it could do this – 1+3=4/2=2. So, your model would calculate the average of oranges and beef as being cauliflower. Based on that, the correlations are going to be hopelessly wrong and that is where one-hot encoding saves the day.

Instead of labeling from 1 upwards for each of our categories, we can opt for binary-style. To start with, look at a visual example of the difference between label encoding and one-hot and see if you can spot the difference:

Label Encoding:

Food Name	Categorical #	Calories
Orange	1	101
Beef	2	275
Cauliflower	3	65

One-Hot Encoding:

Orange	Beef	Cauliflower	Calories
1	0	0	101
0	1	0	275
0	0	1	65

So, can you see the difference? In the first example, with label encoding, we had our categories in rows but, with one-hot encoding, they are in columns. The numerical variable, in our case, calories, does not change. Where there is a 1 in a column, the computer knows which category the row data is in. In short, each category now has an extra binary column.

It isn't clear right off the bat why this is a better solution and that's because there is no clear reasoning. Like a lot of things on deep learning, you won't use one-hot encoding all the time; it isn't better than label encoding, it just works better for some things, problems that you will come across with label encoding and categorical data.

One-Hot Encoding Examples

Theory is great but, sometimes, things are much clearer when you see code. This is not a practical example, merely a way for you to see how things are done. For this example, we need to import some libraries – NumPy, pandas, and sklearn:

```
from sklearn.preprocessing import LabelEncoder, OneHotEncoder
import numpy as np
import pandas as pd
```

With the tools at hand, we can get to work. Our dataset is a made-up one and we use the .read_csv feature in pandas to input the dataset:

```
dataset = pd.read_csv('made_up_thing.csv')
```

That should be self-explanatory, but things get a little more complex from here. Spreadsheets are funny things; they may contain columns of data that you really don't have any interest in while others will contain all the information you want. We're going to use all the columns except the final one and we'll use another pandas feature, .iloc, to get the data from the column we want:

```
X = dataset.iloc[:, :-1].values
```

The .iloc feature takes both [rows, columns] so our input was [:,:-1]. The use of : is telling iloc that we want every row from the columns specified. .values will get the values from the specified segments so, in easy terms, the first bit chooses the values, the second gets them.

Now we can do some encoding, and this is easy with sklearn. There is, however, a small catch. Earlier, we imported the labelencoder, but we also imported the one-hot encoder. The one-hot encoder in sklearn has no clue about converting categories into numbers; all it can do is convert the numbers into binary so that means the labelencoder has to be used first.

So, the first thing to do, as you would a normal object, is set up the labelencoder:

le = LabelEncoder()

Then we need the .fit_transform function from sklearn. For this example, we will encode only the first column:

X[:, 0] = le.fit_transform(X[:, 0])

This is just the .fit and the .transform commands combined. .fit will take X (we specify just the first column of X) and convert all that is in the column into numerical data. Then .transform will apply the conversion.

That just leaves us with the one-hot encoder to use and it isn't much different to what we already did:

ohe = OneHotEncoder(categorical_features = [0])
X = ohe.fit_transform(X).toarray()

The parameter of categorical_features specifies the column that needs to be one-hot encoded; in our case, we want the first column, so we specify [0]. Lastly, fit_transform is used to go to a binary and then into an array that we can easily work with in the future.

That really is all there is to it, it's that simple. There is one thing of note though; if you want to encode more columns, you do the exact same thing but, rather than 0, you specify the column numbers. If you want to encode multiple columns, you could use a for loop:

```
le = LabelEncoder()#for 10 columns
for i in range(10):
    X[:,i] = le.fit_transform(X[:,i])
```

Introducing Word Embeddings

Another popular and effective way to associate a vector with a phrase is the use of thick word vectors, known as word embedding. While one-hot vectors are binary, sparse (most of which are nil and very high), the word vectors coding are low dimensional vectors, i.e. vectors that are dense in comparison with spartan ones. Vectors have a dense dimension. Conversely, word embedding is learned from information, as compared with word vectors acquired through one-hot encryption. In very large vocabulary Word embedding is common and has a dimension of 256, 512 or 1,024. One-hot encoding words, on the contrary most at times lead to vectors of 20,000-dimensional or higher vectors (in this situation, a 20,000-tokens vocabulary is used). Word embedding packages more data in much smaller sizes.

One-hot word vectors are usually sparse, have a large number of dimensions, and are usually coded into the system. Word embedding on the other hand are dense, tend to have low dimensions and are mostly learned directly from the data.

There are two main methods of getting the embeddings of words:

- Learn term embedding in conjunction with the primary assignment (such as the classification of documents and prediction of sentiment). In this setup you begin with random word vectors and then you learn the weights of a neural network by the same way as word vectors.

- Use a distinct machine-learning job to load into your model word embedding than the one you are attempting to find. This is known as pre-trained word inserts.

Let's have a close peek at both.

Using The Embedding Layer

Choosing the vector at random is the easiest way to associate the dense vector with a phrase. The issue here is that there is no structure in the resulting room: for example, words such as 'right' and 'correct' could end up categorized in completely distinct embeddings though in real practice they can very easily replace each other when used in sentences. A deep neural network seems to not work efficiently when applied to such a noisy, unstructured integration space. The geometric links between word vectors should represent the semantic interactions between these phrases to become a bit more abstract. Word embedding is intended as a geometric room to map human language. In a reasonable space, for example, synonyms can be expected to be embedded in like word vectors; and in general, A semantic distance between the associated terms should be linked to the measured geometric distance (as L2) between any two word vectors (words that have various meanings are embedded in points away from one another, where the associated words are closed). You may wish to see specific guidelines in relation to the scope of the embedding region.

Let's look at a practical example to clarify this.

Imagine we were to place the following four words which are embedded in a 2D plane: boy, girl, man, and woman. By virtue of the way we have chosen our vectors to be represented, some structural relationships these words share can be very easily encoded as though they were geometric transformations. For instance, say there's a vector that is said to link the word "boy" to the word "man" and that the very same vector also acts as a link between the word "girl" and the word "woman", then it won't be inaccurate to describe such a vector as a "from younger to older" vector. Conversely, say there's a vector that is said to link the word "boy" to the word "girl" and that the very same vector also acts as a link between the word "man" and the word "woman", then it won't be inaccurate to describe such a vector as "from male to female" vector.

Common examples of significant geometric transformations in word-integrating spaces in the real world are "gender" and "plural" vectors. For example, we get a vector 'hen' by adding the 'female' vector to the 'cock' vector. We get 'cocks' by adding the 'plural' vector. Word embedding places typically includes a whole lot of such interpretable, potentially vital vectors. Does any room exist for word embedding completely capable of mapping the languages of humans and being made use of during a natural language problem? Maybe, but we still have something like that to calculate. Furthermore, there is no such thing as a human language: many distinct languages are present and are not isomorphic because a language reflects a particular culture and context. More pragmatically, however, what creates a healthy room for word-integration largely relies on the assignment: the ideal place for word-integration for an English-worded sentiment analytics model may differ from that for an English-worded model for the legal-documents-classification system, since the significance of different semantic relations differs from problem to problem.

It is therefore sensible for each fresh job to learn new embedding spaces. Fortunately, backpropagation facilitates this and Keras facilitates it. We need to learn the weight of the layer: the layer Embedding.

```
# Create new Embedding layer
from keras.layers import Embedding

embedding_layer = Embedding(1000, 64)
```

In our model, the embedding layer is designed to receive at least two arguments which are: 1) the number of possible tokens (in our case, 1,000: 1 + the largest word index) and 2) the dimensionality of the embeddings (in this case, 64).

The best way to understand the Embedding layer is probably as a sort of dictionary that maps integer indices (which take the place of specific words) to dense vectors. It requires the inputs, searches for those integers and returns the related vectors to an inner dictionary. It is a dictionary search efficiently.

Word Index To Embedding Layer To Corresponding Word Vector

The Embedding layer is given a 2D integer in the form of an integer, i.e. sampling, sequence length. In the tensor, each entry is a sequence of integers. It is possible to embed sequences of varying length, such as the shaped batches we used in earlier examples – (32, 10) which equates to 32 sequences each of length 10 – and these can be fed to a built-in layer. However, because they must go into a single tensor, all of the batch sequences must be the same size – any smaller sequence must be zeroed, and larger ones must be truncated. A 3D floating-point tensor in the form of (samples, length of sequence, embedded dimensionality) is returned by the layer and this can then be handled by a 1D convolution layer or an RNN layer. When an embedding layer is installed, the weights are random, just as they are with other layers. The word vectors are gradually adapted through a process of back-spreading and the room is structured in a way that the downstream model can be used. Once full training has been completed, there a great deal of structure in the integration area and this structure is specific to the problem you trained your model for.

We can make use of this concept to do some sentiment-work prediction on the IMDB film review dataset. The information is prepared first – we restrict the film reviews to 10,000 common words and the cut-off point will be 20 phrases. For every set of 10,000 words, the model learns eight-dimensional embeddings. The 2D tensor, which is the entry integer sequence, is transformed into an embedded sequence, which is a 3D tensor; the tensor is then flattened to a 2D tensor and Dense layer is drawn to the top.

```
# Load IMDB data for use with Embedding layer
from keras.datasets import imdb
from keras import preprocessing

# Number of words considered as features
max_features = 10000
# The text is stopped after this number
# of words (among the max_features most common words)
maxlen = 20

# The data is loaded as lists of integers
(x_train, y_train), (x_test, y_test) =
imdb.load_data(num_words=max_features)

# The lists of integers are transformed into a 2D integer
# tensor of shape (samples, maxlen)
x_train = preprocessing.sequence.pad_sequences(x_train,
maxlen=maxlen
x_test = preprocessing.sequence.pad_sequences(x_test,
maxlen=maxlen)
```

Using An Embedding Layer And Classifier On The IMDB Data

The maximum entry duration for the Embedding layer is specified, so that integrated inputs can then be flattened. Activations are formed (specimens, maxlen, 8) after the embedment layer.

```
from keras.models import Sequential
from keras.layers import Flatten, Dense

model = Sequential()
model.add(Embedding(10000, 8, input_length=maxlen))
# Flattens 3D tensor of embeddings into a 2D
# tensor of shape (samples, maxlen * 8)
model.add(Flatten())
# Adds classifier on top
model.add(Dense(1, activation='sigmoid'))
model.compile(optimizer='rmsprop',      loss='binary_crossentropy',
metrics=['acc'])
model.summary()
history = model.fit(x_train, y_train,
                    epochs=10,
                    batch_size=32,
                    validation_split=0.2)
```

The validation precision is approximately 76 percent, which is great given that in each review you only look at the first 20 phrases. Note, however, that just flattening the integrated sections and training the Dense layer above takes us to a model which treats every word individually within the input tensor, without regard for the inter-word interactions and phrase structure (for instance, this model could consider "this cinema is a bomb" as well as "this film is a bomb" as adverse reviews). In addition to the integrated sequences, it is far more efficient to add recurring levels or 1-dimensional convolutional layers to learn functionalities which take each sequence into consideration. This is something we will dig deep into in the next few sections.

Making Use Of Word Embeddings That Have Been Trained

You can sometimes get so little training data that it would not be feasible to use the data as-is to learn a suitable task-based vocabulary embedding. So, what are you going to do in that case? In such a situation, it will be useful to load the built-in vector in a pre-trained embedding space, which has been designed to be very well structured and has a lot of useful properties aimed at capturing the generic elements of linguistic composition, instead of studying word embedding together with the issue you are working on fixing. The reason behind using pre-trained word embedding in problems that involve natural language processing is much the same as the idea behind the classification of images by means of pre-trained neural networks: You do not have a lot of data at your disposal, but you also need the characteristics to be relatively generic–that is, prevalent visual characteristics of semantic characteristics –to learn genuinely strong characteristics by themselves. In this situation, reusing characteristics learned about another issue makes sense.

The word embeddings are computed by measuring how frequently they occur, along with other important statistics, using several different methods, some of which include neural networks. The concept of the space for the small-format word embedding was first studied by Bengio et al in the early 2000s but this was soon followed by the creation of the Word2vec algorithm, one of the most successful and most-used word integration systems, by Tomas Mikolov from Google. That algorithm is used for capturing semantic features, like gender.

To implement the embedding layer from Keras, there are several word embedding databases that have already been computed for you, one of which is Word2vec. Another popular one is called GloVe, or Global Word Representation Vectors, which was created by Stanford scientists in 2014., and is based on matrices of co-occurrent word statistics. And there are also integrations pre-computed by the Wikipedia and Common Cravl information systems, containing millions of accessible English tokens.

We can see the approach the Keras model takes to initiate and implement GloVe embedding and the same approach works for any other similar integration database such as Word2vec. This instance is also going to be used for refreshing the text tokenization technique that we talked about earlier in the guide.

Summary

In the course of this chapter, we have made use of examples which have gone through various important steps involved in the building of effective deep learning systems, from computer vision systems to text analyzing systems. As the topic suggests, this book is aimed at being an introduction into the practice of deep learning using the

Python programming language, and the reader is therefore advised to complement the knowledge gotten here by reading up blogs, seeing video tutorials, but most importantly, by having a particular project in mind and learning all it takes to solve it on-the-fly. This is definitely a technique I recommend, and which seems to work for a lot of deep learning professionals. Simply following tutorials will not suffice. In order to hone the skills gotten here, you need to try solving a problem you actually want to solve.

Chapter 6

Other Real World Applications of Deep Learning

The conventional machine learning makes use of handwritten extraction feature and also machine learning systems that are modality-specific to give labels to images and recognize voices. This method, however, has several inconveniences in terms of timeliness and precision. The advanced deep learning neural networks available today make use of algorithms, a huge amount of data and the GPU's computing power to solve this problem.

Deep learning is a way of simulating two human senses, those of hearing and sight. Because of this, there are many applications, as there are uses, for understanding images and sound. Some use cases of deep learning include:

Image Recognition:

- **Image Tagging** - Facebook, for example, contains hundreds of thousands of photographs used for training algorithms automated by a Facebook friend uploading an image and tagging others in it.

- **Identifying Items in Real-Time** – along with recognizing those that are blind or visually impaired just by using a smartphone app. One such app is called Aipoly, an iOS app that makes use of software that was trained on the Teradeep Deep Learning Software convolutional network – the dataset used contains around 10 million images.

- **Recreating Old Masters Paintings** – a group of researchers from a German institution called the University of Tubingen have developed an algorithm capable of transforming any image so it looks as though it is in an old Masters painting, in the style of a specific Master.

- **Drug Discovery** – Deep learning has brought about the revolution of medical diagnosis, through the use of algorithms trained on images. The Butterfly Network, for example, was developed to allow anyone access to medical imaging, no matter where they are in the world. It is just one deep learning application that will lead to many lives being saved.

- **OCR** – Optical Character Recognition – this deep learning problem is an image processing subset, developed to allow computers to take an image, process it and extract the text contained in it. This text is then correlated with the corresponding image object.

- **Emotion Detection** – deep learning is now perfectly able to detect a range of emotions on human faces using images and/or videos. One such program is called Affectiva and it is a subset of the MIT Media Lab.

- **Brand Tracking** – deep learning can also be used for tracking brands at events, making comparisons between the brand and its rivals and targeting ad campaigns to identify logos and brands for specific companies in images on multiple social media sites.

Natural Language Processing

Deep learning implemented to recognize speech

- Deep learning is being used in Speech Recognition devices aimed at searches that are to be voice driven. Popular examples of these are Android OS, Siri and Cortana.

- Conversation analysis: Deep learning is being used to accurately identify individual speakers in a conversation, vital words employed in the conversation, and depending on how good, is able to detect pivotal parts of the conversation, and the total time over which the conversation was carried out, they are also capable of selecting take away points for each group involved in large meetings such as conference calls. Gridspace makes for a good example of companies aiming at maximizing conversational awareness in communications.

Language Translation

- Natural Language Processing is a deep learning technology which Google uses in its Google Translate mobile applications. Google Translate is capable of extracting and recognizing text found in images and is capable of making translations from whatever language the text exists, to about 20 other languages.

Speech-to-Text (transcription)

- Processing text from human speech - Natural Language Processing (NLP) is being effectively used in the transcription of voices, and these transcriptions are made available to speakers of a very wide range of language (which of course, it detects).

Text-to-speech systems

- Django is a floating helper running on your telephone and forecasting emoji, stickers, and GIFs based on what you and your colleagues in any app write. It means Django needs to understand the meaning of what you write to suggest emoji that you might like to use. Emoji is difficult to suggest. See Django's engineering here.

Drug Discovery

- Deep neural networks that have been trained in the field of large sets of transcriptional response data may classify different medicines into therapeutic categories based solely on the basis of their transcriptional profiles (here are papers about the pharmacology of drugs for deep learning)

- Deep learning excelled in the forecast of toxicity and exceeded many computer methods such as Bayes and random forests. The Institute of Bioinformatics has shown that deep learning is excellent in carrying out this task.

- Understanding illnesses, genetic therapies: how natural and therapeutic variations in genetic engineering change the cellular process such as DNA-to-RNA transcription, splicing, etc.

Consumer Relations

- Publicity for Brands: The use of deep knowledge enables advertisers and marketers to define the correct audience to target social platforms and propose to clients on the basis of information (Affinio for instance)

- Grouping of Audience: Social audiences are segmented across multiple platforms, based on the uncontrolled identification and segmentation of naturally growing tribes and the uniqueness of these tribes.

- Recommenders for Content: Once particular sections of the public have been recognized, they suggest content (themes, sentences, text, pictures, videos, etc.) that brands generate on the basis of what they are discussing, sharing, publishing and examining.

- Efficient and Effective Advertisement: The combination of natural segmentation and content recommendations to suggest who is intended to be used for publicity design as well as keywords, images, etc.

- Prediction of Sponsorships: Deep education can be implemented to find out precisely how often during a sports case a particular brand appears.

Recommender systems

i. Mining Sentiment Analysis and Opinion: The analysis of sentiments, also referred to as Opinion Mining, is an application of deep learning with the aim of examining the opinions, feelings, assessments, attitudes and emotions of people, for instance of products, departments, organizations, individuals, issues, events, topics and their attributes. It is a huge issue area. An interesting article on this subject here

ii. Automatic music recommendation can be addressed by deep learning which has become a growing issue in recent years, because a large part of the music is now digitally sold and consumed.

iii. Detection of subjectivity, classification of words, classification of document feelings, and extraction of view.

Game Play

- Atari games are learned by artificial intelligence. The Atari expert is an algorithm for the deep learning of DQN. The DQN learning algorithm for general use might be the first step on a ladder to artificial intelligence.

Fraud Detection

- Continuous methodological development is an essential feature of online fraud. Tens of thousands of latent functionalities (time signals, performers, and geo-locations are simple instances) which could constitute a specific fraud and even can detect' sub modus operandi' or various versions in the same system could be analyzed with in-depth learning algorithms.

Autonomous Driving

- Crash-prevention devices and experimental driverless vehicles today depend on radar and other sensors for the detection of roadside pedestrians. However, a vision-based security system in vehicles has remained unusual, as computers typically face a compromise between rapid video analyze and drawing the correct findings. A foot-and-mouth detection scheme based on deep neural networks can work on the basis of visual evidence alone and improve the current strategy closely in real-time.

- By circumventing hard-coding the detection of particular characteristics — such as lane markings, railings, or other vehicles — and by preventing the creation of an almost endless amount of "if not, then" coding statements, which are too inappropriate in attempting to account for the randomness of DAVE2 highways

Anomaly Detection

Malware has become more and more hard to recognize through signature and heuristic techniques, which mean that most antivirus (AV) programs are unfortunately useless in the fight against malware mutation. Typical malware comprises of approximately 10,000 code lines. Changing just 1% of the code will make most AVs ineffective. Deep Instinct applies artificial intelligence Deep Learning algorithms to detect structures and program functions that are indicative of malware.

Create your own case: Nervana gives you a deep learning framework called Neon that enables you to create your own case through deep learning networks and a cloud service to import and evaluate information through deep study templates.

Giving the following fields among many others the capacity to see and hear will affect them deeply:

1. **Medicine/Surgery**: An enormous amount of progress is being made in robotic surgery, based on highly delicate tactile materials. However, if a doctor is able to advise a robot to "move a split mm remaining of the clavicle," they may achieve greater control by guiding the robot via the complete comprehensive voice control system.

2. **Driving** – we already have self-driving cars and deep learning is likely to integrate into automated driving systems, so that sights and sounds beyond the human capacity can be detected and interpreted.

3. **Military**: The use of drones by the military is another unsurprising development. Military drones and other devices powered by deep learning are being deployed to help strengthen the security of the nation.

4. **Surveillance**: Deep learning is being increasingly used for the purpose of surveillance. Sometimes drones are used for the purpose of surveillance, but the active development of systems that will be given the ability to sense and (with an uncanny degree of precision similar to that of humans) interpret its surrounding environment is sure to make great changes in the operation of the field of surveillance.

Projections Of The Future Applications Of Deep Learning

The way deep learning resolves long-standing human problems through visualization and understanding and reading in context, these ideas can in the future be applied in many areas. Those ideas can be applied. These issues can be solved in the near future with enormous deep learning skills.

1. Conversational cues: Imagine you find yourself in the middle of a discussion where you know little to nothing about the topic at hand, by the use of deep learning, you now have the option to activate your smartphone application, and the system will begin to listen in on that meeting, and if you desire, is capable of making suggestions, giving you the chance to actually contribute to this discussion which is on a topic you knew

nothing about prior to that. This is the world our kids will certainly live in. And very likely, we will too.

2. Suggesting actions based on mood- your app might know you so well based on your recent conversation, messages, time of the day and recent developments in your life it might suggest you real-life actions like watching movies, working out, calling a friend etc. more like a close friend.

So deep learning, working with other algorithms, can help with classifying, clustering and prediction, with accuracies far above those of humans. This is achieved automatically by knowing the signals or structure in the information. When they train deep learning algorithms, they devise the information, evaluate their mistakes against given training set and go on to correct their way of making guesses to be more precise.

Now imagine that with a lot of learning, any data on your images, video, sound, text and DNA, time series (touch, bursary, economic tables, weather) may be classified, grouped or predicted. Anything people can feel and can be digitized by our technology. Basically, we give society with deep learning the capacity to be much smarter by interpreting precisely what is going on around the globe in terms of software.

Deep Learning Glossary of Terms

As you have probably discovered, some of the terminologies that surround deep learning can be overwhelming. In this glossary I have listed the most common terms to help you understand them better and to give you a quick guide that you can glance at whenever you need to. The line between deep learning and machine learning technology is somewhat blurred so I have tried to include terms that only apply to deep learning here and not to machine learning in general.

A

Activation Function

Nonlinear activation functions are applied to some layers of a neural network to allow it to learn the complex decision boundaries. The most common activation functions are tanh, sigmoid, ReLU, and other variants of them.

Adadelta

Adadelta is a learning algorithm based on gradient descent; it adapts its own learning rate, over time, for each parameter. It was originally developed to improve on Adagrad, an algorithm that is far more parameter-sensitive and may be a little too aggressive in decreasing leaning rates.

Adagrad

An algorithm with an adaptive learning rate, Adagrad tracks squared gradients over a period of time and adapts its per-parameter learning rate automatically. It is useful for cases of sparse data where it can assign the parameters that are not updated very often with a higher rate of learning.

Adam

Another of the algorithms with an adaptive learning rate, it estimates updates directly by making use of a running average of the gradient's first and second moment and adding in a term to correct the bias.

Affine Layer

An affine layer is a fully connected neural network layer. The name 'affine' indicates that every neuron in the preceding layer is connected to one in the current layer. This is, in most ways, a standard neural network layer. Affine layers tend to be added over the outputs in a CNN or RNN before the final prediction is made. Typically, the affine layer is in this format – $y = f(Wx + b)$ in which x indicates the layer input, W indicates the parameters, b indicates a bias vector and f indicates a nonlinear activation function.

Attention Mechanism

Inspired by visual attention in humans, attention mechanisms are able to focus attention on a certain part of a given image. They can be used in image recognition and in language processing to give a helping hand to the network in learning where its focus should be for predictions.

Alexnet

The CNN architecture that took first place in the ILSVRC competition in 2012, winning by a long streak and resulting in an interest in CNNs used for recognition being rekindled. Alexnet is made up of five convolutional layers, with some of them preceding a max-pooling layer, along with three fully connected layers and one 1000-way softmax.

Autoencoder

Autoencoders are neural network models with the goal of using a bottleneck in the network to predict the input. The bottleneck makes the network learn a representation of the input with lower dimensions. In effect this compresses it down to a 'good' representation. The autoencoder is related to dimensionality reduction but because it is nonlinear, it is able to learn mappings that are more complex.

Average-Pooling

One of the pooling techniques in the CNN for image recognition, average-pooling works by placing a window over specified sections of features, i.e. the pixels, and then averaging the values inside the window. The input representation is compressed to one that is lower in dimension.

B

Backpropagation

This algorithm is used for the efficient calculation of neural network gradients. It applies the differentiation chain rule, beginning from the network output and propagating the gradients back.

Backpropagation Through Time (BPTT)

Much like standard backpropagation, the BPTT algorithm is a standard one that we apply to RNNs. Each individual time step represents a single layer and the parameters get shared across every single layer. RNNs share parameters with every time step, meaning any errors at any one of those steps will need to be backpropagated through time to every step that preceded it. When you have a lot of inputs in one long sequence, a shortened version of BPTT can be used to keep the computational costs as low as possible – using this means only the errors for a given number of steps will be backpropagated.

Batch Normalization

This technique is used for normalizing the layer inputs for each mini-batch. It speeds training up significantly which means higher learning rates can be used, and it acts as a regularizer. It is highly effective for both feedforward and convolutional neural networks but has not yet been successful on RNNs.

Bidirectional RNN

A Bidirectional RNN is a neural network containing two RNNs, each one going in opposing directions. The forward RNN takes the input sequence and reads it from start to finish while the backward RNN reads in the opposite direction. The RNNs are both stacked and, normally, their states are combined by appending the vectors. Bidirectional RNNs are useful for NLP tasks where predictions are made by taking context from before and after a word.

C

Caffe

One of the most popular of all the deep learning frameworks, Caffe performs very well on both vision problems and CNN models.

Categorical Cross-Entropy Loss

Also called the negative log-likelihood, categorical cross-entropy loss is one of the most popular of the loss functions for categorization. The function takes two probability distributions and measures any similarity between them – the distributions are usually the true labels and the predicted ones. The function takes the form of $L = -\text{sum}(y * \log(y\_prediction))$ in which y is the true label probability (a one-hot vector) and the predicted label probability is indicated by y_prediction.

Channel

Deep learning models may have multiple channels through which the input data is fed. Canonical examples include images, which have the RGB channels (red, green, blue). 3F tensors can be sued to represent images with each dimension corresponding to, respectively, channel, height, width. There may also be multiple channels in natural language data, for example, different embedding types.

Convolutional Neural Network (CNN, ConvNet)

CNN's extract features from an input's local regions using convolutions. Most models will be a combination of pooling, convolution, and affine layers and, over time, they have proved very popular, particularly on tasks involving visual recognition, due to their high performance.

D

Deep Belief Network (DBN)

A DBN is a 'probabilistic graphical' deep learning model which can learn hierarchical representations of data, unsupervised. They are made up of several hidden layers, the neurons connected in successive layer pairs. A DBN is a stack of RBNs, each trained one at a time.

Deep Dream

Deep Dream is a Google technique that attempts to extract knowledge that a deep CNN has captured. This technique is able to transform images that already exist giving them a dreamlike feel when it is recursively applied, or it is able to generate some new images.

Dropout

A regularization technique used on neural networks. Dropout prevents the occurrence of overfitting by stopping the neurons from adapting together. This is done by setting a small portion of the neurons to 0 at every training iteration. We can interpret dropout in a few ways, including taking random samples from an expanding number of networks. Very popular with CNNs, dropout is also proving worthy of use for other layers, such as the RNNs and input embeddings.

E

Embedding

Embeddings are used to map input representations into vectors, i.e. sentences or individual words. One of the most popular embedding types is word embeddings, like GloVe and Word2vec. It is also possible to embed images, paragraphs and sentences, i.e. if we map imaged and their descriptions (text) to common embedding spaces and make the distance as small as possible between them, labels can be matched to images. There are two ways to learn embeddings –

explicitly, like with Word2vec or in supervised tasks, like Sentiment Analysis. More often than not, a network's input layer is initialized using embeddings that have already been trained; these are fine-tuned to cope with the specific task.

Exploding Gradient Problem

The polar opposite of the Vanishing Gradient problems. In a DNN, it is possible for gradients to explode while being backpropagated and the result is an overflow of numbers. Gradient clipping is one way of dealing with these exploding gradients.

F

Fine-Tuning

Fine-tuning is a technique whereby a network is initialized suing the parameters from a different task; the parameters are then updated as per the task they are being used for. NLP architecture, for example, tends to make use of word embeddings already trained, such as word2vec; during training the embeddings are updated based on the specific task they will be doing.

G

Gradient Clipping

A common technique used for the prevention of exploding gradients in DNNs, usually in RNNs. There are a number of ways that gradient clipping can be performed but the most common technique is normalizing a parameter vector's gradients when the

L2 norm goes over a threshold specified in new_gradients = gradients * threshold / l2_norm(gradients).

GloVe

An unsupervised learning algorithm, GloVe is used to get embeddings, or vector representations, for words. The vectors have the exact same function as the word2vec vectors but the vector representations are different because co-occurrence statistics are used to train them.

GoogleLeNet

The CNN architecture that took first place in the ILSVRC in 2014. It reduces parameters by using inception modules, improving the way computational resources are used in the network.

GRU

GRU, or Gated Recurrent Unit, is like an LSTM unit but much simpler and having fewer parameters. Similar to the LSTM cell, a gating mechanism is used to let the RNN learn, efficiently, the long-range dependency. It does this by stopping the problem of vanishing gradients. GRUs have both reset and update gates used for working out which bits of the old memory should be kept or updated with updated values when it reaches the current time step.

H

Highway Layer

Highway layers are a kind of neural network layers that make use of gating mechanisms to control how information flows through layers. It is possible to stack these layers one on top of another to train the very deep networks. A highway layer will learn the gate function that picks the bits of the input that need to be passed through and the bits that are passed through transformation functions. A highway layer basic formulation is $T * h(x) + (1 - T) * x$; T is the gating function that is learned (with values of 0 to 1); the input transformation is $h(x)$ and the input is x. All must be of the same size.

I

ILSVRC

A challenge that takes place every year, the ImageNet Large Scale Visual Recognition Challenge evaluates image classification and object detection algorithms at a large scale. It is an incredibly popular computer vision challenge and has resulted in deep learning techniques that, over time, have shown significant error rate reductions, from 30% down to below 5%; some of these techniques have beaten humans on a large number of classification tasks.

Inception Module

Used in CNNs to ensure computation is more efficient and uses dimensionality reduction in deeper networks using 1 x 1 stacked convolutions.

K
Keras

Keras is a popular deep learning library in Python. It is full of building blocks for the DNNs and can be run on CNTK, TensorFlow, or Theano.

L
LSTM

A Long Short-Term Memory network that uses gating mechanisms to stop vanishing gradients in RNNs. When we use LSTM units for calculating an RNNs hidden state, the network can propagate the gradients more efficiently and it can learn the long-range dependencies.

M
Max-Pooling

Max-pooling is an operation usually used in CNNs. The max-pooling layer will choose the biggest value from feature patches and like the convolutional layer, window size and stride size are used as its parameters. i.e. a window of 2 x 2 size may be slid over a feature matrix of 10 x 10 using a size 2 stride; it selects the biggest values (max) across the values in each of the windows and the result is a new feature matrix of x 5. Pooling layers can reduce a representation's dimensionality by the information considered to be the most important. With image inputs, the pooling layer provides translation with basic invariance, which means that, even moving the image by a number of pixels, the same max values are selected. Max-pooling layers tend to be placed in between a succession of convolutional layers.

MNIST

MNIST is a common dataset used for image recognition. It has 70,000 examples of handwritten digits split into 60,000 examples for training and 10,000 examples for testing. Every image is exactly 28 x 28 pixels and the best models tend to achieve a minimum of 99.5% accuracy.

Momentum

This extends the Gradient Descent algorithm and either damps or accelerates the updates to the parameters. In practical terms, if you add a momentum term into the GDA updates, you get much better rates of convergence in DNNs.

Multilayer Perceptron (MLP)

A type of Feedforward neural network, an MLP has several layers that are fully connected, each using a nonlinear activation function for dealing with non-linearly separable data. MLPs are a very basic form of multilayer neural networks or if there are more than two layers, of deep neural networks.

N

Negative Log-Likelihood (NLL)

Refer to Categorical Cross Entropy Loss

Neural Machine Translation (NMT)

NMT systems make use of a neural network for translating between two languages, like English and German. End-to-end training is done with bilingual corpora, different from standard machine learning systems used for translation which need engineering and features that are hand-crafted. Encoder and decoder RNNS are usually used to implement an NMT for both encoding the sentence and for decoding and producing the result.

Neural Turing Machine (NTM)

An NTM is a neural network architecture that takes examples and infers a simple algorithm. As an example, an NTM can take sample inputs and sample outputs and learn sorting algorithms from them. They usually learn a kind of 'memory-and-attention' system for dealing with state while a program is being executed.

Nonlinearity

Refer to Activation Function

Noise-Contrastive Estimation (NCE)

NCE is a kind of sampling loss which is normally used for training classifiers that have large output vocabularies. It is too expensive in computation terms to calculate a softmax on huge numbers of possible classes so, with NCE, the problem can be reduced to binary classification – the classifier is trained to discriminate between noise distribution that is generated artificially and samples from real distributions.

P

Pooling

Refer to Max-Pooling

R

Restricted Boltzmann Machine (RBN)

An RBM is a kind of probabilistic graphical model. It could be interpreted as being a stochastic artificial neural network and they are used for unsupervised learning of data representations. RBMs are made up of a visible layer, a hidden layer, and in each layer the connections between the binary neurons.

Recurrent Neural Network (RNN)

RNNs are used or modeling sequential interactions through memory or a hidden state. They are able to take up to N inputs and they can also produce N outputs. I.e. you may have a sentence as an input sequence – the outputs are the part-of-speech tags for each individual word. You could have a sentence as an input with a sentiment classification for that sentence as the output. A single mage could be the input with a sequence of words that correspond to the image description. An RNN will calculate new memory or hidden state at every time step, based on what the previous hidden state was and the current network. The 'recurrent' part of it comes in because the same parameters get used at each step and the network will do the same calculations but based on the different inputs.

Recursive Neural Network

A recursive neural network is a generalization of an RNN to tree-like structures. At each of the recursions, the same weights get applies and, like an RNN, end-to-end training is possible with backpropagation. While the tree structure may be learned as a part of an optimization problem, a recursive neural network is usually applied to the problems that already have a structure, such as parse trees in NLP.

ReLU

Rectified Linear Units, or ReLUs tend to be used in DNNs as activation function and are defined by the form $f(x) = max(0, x)$. They do have advantages over other functions like tanh; they are sparse, i.e. activation can be set to 0 easily, and they don't tend to suffer from vanishing gradients so much either. They are commonly used in CNNs and there are a few variations, such as PReLU (Parametric ReLU and Leaky ReLUs.

ResNet

Winner of the ILSVRC challenge in 2015, Deep Residual Networks, or ResNet for short, works by providing a shortcut connection over a stack of layers. This gives the optimizer the opportunity to learn residual mappings that are much easier than the originals which are quite complicated. They are a bit like the highway layers but are not dependent on data and no extra training complexity or parameters are introduced.

RMSProp

One of the gradient-based optimization algorithms, RMSProp is much like Adagrad but with an extra decay term which counteracts the rapid learning rate decrease in Adagrad.

S

Seq2Seq

Seq2Seq or Sequence-to-Sequence models read sequences as inputs and produce an output of another sequence. They are different from RNNs because the input is read entirely before any output is produced. Usually, two RNNS are used to implement this, an encoder and a decoder. One common example of the seq2seq model is neural machine translation (NMT).

SGD

SGD is a gradient-based algorithm for optimization and is otherwise known as Stochastic Gradient Descent. The algorithm is used for learning network parameters in training and the backpropagation algorithm is used for calculating the gradients. Generally, mini-batch versions are used, in which the updates to the parameters are done based on batches and not on single examples. This leads to more efficient computation.

Softmax

Softmax is a function usually used for converting vectors containing raw scores into class probabilities. This is generally done at the output layer in classification neural networks. The function will normalize the scores though a process of exponentiation and division by a normalization constant If the number of classes is large, it is very expensive to compute the constant.

T

TensorFlow

An open-source software library for Python and C++, uses data flow graphs for numerical computation. Google created TensorFlow and it is not dissimilar to Theano although it isn't as high-level as Keras or Caffe.

Theano

Another Python library, Theano allows for the definition, optimization, and evaluation of mathematical expressions. There are a lot of building blocks in it for DNNs and it is a low-level library.

V

Vanishing Gradient Problem

This problem is found most often in the really deep neural networks, usually RNNs, or those that make use of activation functions with small gradients. As the gradients tend to be multiplied in the backpropagation, they 'vanish' as they go through the layers and this prevents the leaning of long-range dependency. Activation functions that do not have small gradients (such as ReLU) or LSTMs can be used to combat this problem.

VGG

A CNN model that took the top two places in the ILSVRC challenge in 2014 for localization and classification. The model is made up of between 1 and 19 weight layers and makes use of convolutional filters that are quite small, 1 x1 an 3 x 3.

W

word2vec

An algorithm used for learning word embedding by attempting to predict word content in documents. The word vectors that result have some properties that are quite interesting. Two objectives can be used for learning the embeddings – the CBOW objective, which attempts to predict words from their context and the Skip-Gram objective, which attempts to predict the context from words.

Conclusion

In this book, we have taken a deep dive into the world of deep learning, a world which regardless of the hype, truly holds great promises for the future of humanity in terms of an increase in the standard of living. Our journey into this promising field began with the placing of a foundational understanding of the field, by focusing first on its immediate parent field: the field of Machine Learning. In the course of those initial chapters, we built an understanding of Machine Learning, pointing out the difference between its kinds, and from there we dove into the subfield of Neural Networks, the understanding of which is very crucial to the development of a well-rounded knowledge of deep learning. In subsequent chapters of this book, we have gone through several end to end examples of deep learning systems which depending on the efficiency of methods and techniques used, produced predictions with varying degrees of accuracy, which is intended to give guidance as to how the choosing of hyperparameters for your neural network should be carried out.

This was a hands-on book which, if followed carefully, will give the reader the foundational knowledge needed to pursue their personal projects, which should in turn lead to an interesting and hopefully, even financially fulfilling career in the field of deep learning. Serious readers of this book now have the ability to positively affect the world in new and amazing ways. As has been expressed in the book, a good understanding of deep learning has led to the creation of a lot of positive impact by individuals and groups, in ways which were just not possible with the tools that were earlier available to man. Regardless of the amount of foundational knowledge given in this book, it only plays a little role in your journey to become a world-class deep learning practitioner. A small but vital role. The remainder of what will get you there depends on the degree to which you practice the skills taught here, and the advanced topics you are now equipped to learn with ease.

References

http://www.wildml.com

https://blog.algorithmia.com

https://hackernoon.com

https://jjallaire.github.io

https://machinelearningmastery.com

https://medium.com

https://towardsdatascience.com

https://victorzhou.com

https://www.geeksforgeeks.org

https://www.geeksforgeeks.org

https://www.guru99.com

www.ingramcontent.com/pod-product-compliance
Lightning Source LLC
LaVergne TN
LVHW051241050326
832903LV00028B/2510